Isle of Skye
Natural History Walks

Chris Mitchell

© Christopher Mitchell, 2010

All Rights Reserved. No part of this publication may be reproduced, stored in a retrieval system, or transmitted in any form or by any means – electronic, mechanical, photocopying, recording, or otherwise – without prior written permission from the publisher

Published by Sigma Leisure – an imprint of
Sigma Press, Stobart House, Pontyclerc, Penybanc Road
Ammanford, Carmarthenshire SA18 3HP

British Library Cataloguing in Publication Data

A CIP record for this book is available from the British Library

ISBN: 978-1-85058-858-0

Typesetting and Design by: Sigma Press, Ammanford, Carms

Maps: Christopher Mitchell
Maps are based on Ordnance Survey maps: 7th Series, 1:63,360; Sheets 24, 25, 33 and 34 (1956 -1957)

Photographs: Christopher Mitchell (unless otherwise stated)

Front cover: The Old Man of Storr in winter (Walk 3)

Printed by: Akcent Media Limited

Disclaimer: The information in this book is given in good faith and is believed to be correct at the time of publication. Care should always be taken when walking in hill country. Where appropriate, attention has been drawn to matters of safety. The author and publisher cannot take responsibility for any accidents or injury incurred whilst following these walks. Only you can judge your own fitness, competence and experience. Do not rely solely on sketch maps for navigation: we strongly recommend the use of appropriate Ordnance Survey (or equivalent) maps.

Foreword

The Isle of Skye is famous for many reasons, but chief among them is the majestic grandeur of its land and seascapes which provide the perfect antidote for visitors in search of a respite from the pressures of the modern world.

The number of people who flock to Skye each year to experience the island's rich natural and cultural heritage has increased significantly since two of its earliest visitors, Dr. Johnson and James Boswell, made their celebrated tour of the Hebrides in 1773. In his journal, Boswell remarked that they were 'sometimes relieved by a view of branches of the sea, that universal medium of connection amongst mankind' and the 'wild, moorish, hilly and craggy appearances which gave a rude magnificence to the scene.' Although much has changed beyond recognition since then, the magnificent landscape which has inspired generations of writers, artists, climbers and walkers remains one of the few places in Europe where one can access a unique and solitary connection with nature in all its glory.

Chris Mitchell's well-presented and evocative book unlocks the magical secret places to explore and savour on the Isle of Skye.

Hugh MacLeod of MacLeod
Dunvegan Castle and Gardens
Isle of Skye

Acknowledgements

Throughout this whole venture, I have been encouraged by my wife, Janet, who has accompanied me on all the walks and given valuable suggestions and advice at all stages from draft texts to completed manuscript. To her I am, as always, deeply grateful.

My thanks must also go to Frank and Andrew Sharp for checking over several of the routes and for their helpful discussions on the geology of the area; to John, Mike, Cathy, Robert, Anne and Jed for being such worthy companions on many of the walks and for all their help; to members of the Scottish Wildlife Trust (Skye Members' Centre) for sharing their expertise and local knowledge; and to Hugh MacLeod of MacLeod for writing the foreword.

I should also like to acknowledge the late Tom Westman for the flight in his microlight, which enabled me to take the aerial photographs of Oronsay and Macleod's Maidens.

Please note
Many of the features mentioned in this book are in Sites of Special Scientific Interest (SSSIs), are Scheduled Ancient Monuments or important geological sites. Please try and keep disturbance to a minimum and leave plants, rock faces and fossil sites as you found them for others to see.

Most of these walks are across land used for sheep farming. Dogs should therefore be kept on a short leash at all times. This is particularly important during the lambing season during April and May.

By the same author:
Lake District Wet Weather Walks
Lake District Natural History Walks
Peak District Natural History Walks

Contents

Map Key

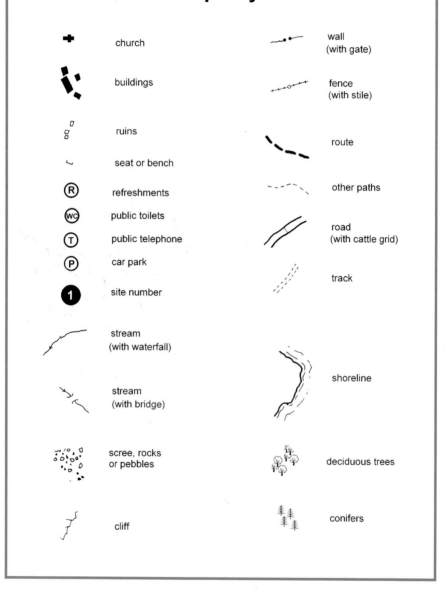

church

buildings

ruins

seat or bench

® refreshments

WC public toilets

T public telephone

P car park

1 site number

stream
(with waterfall)

stream
(with bridge)

scree, rocks
or pebbles

cliff

wall
(with gate)

fence
(with stile)

route

other paths

road
(with cattle grid)

track

shoreline

deciduous trees

conifers

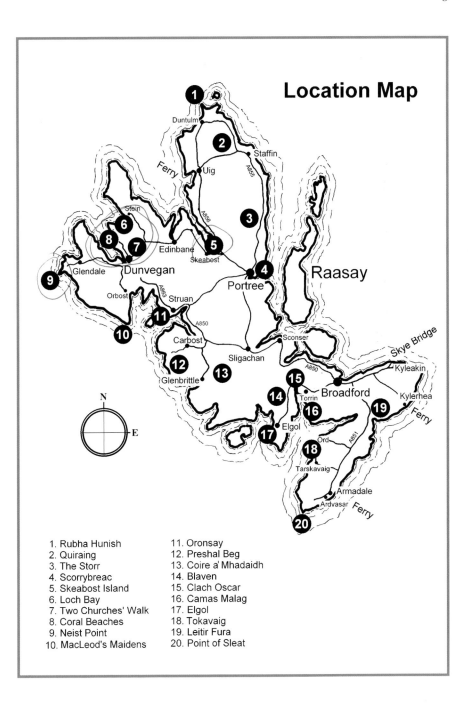

Location Map

1. Rubha Hunish
2. Quiraing
3. The Storr
4. Scorrybreac
5. Skeabost Island
6. Loch Bay
7. Two Churches' Walk
8. Coral Beaches
9. Neist Point
10. MacLeod's Maidens
11. Oronsay
12. Preshal Beg
13. Coire a' Mhadaidh
14. Blaven
15. Clach Oscar
16. Camas Malag
17. Elgol
18. Tokavaig
19. Leitir Fura
20. Point of Sleat

Introduction

For many visitors, the Isle of Skye means rocky scrambles and long walks amongst some of the most dramatic scenery in Britain. What can compare with the Black Cuillin or the Trotternish landslip?

But in the rush to cover distance and reach the summit ridge, so much is often passed by. This book offers an alternative walking guide, focusing on the island's natural history – its rocky shores and limestone pavements, ice-scoured lava flows and acid peat bogs, fertile landslips and ancient woodlands.

Twenty walks have been chosen. And because Nature and Naismith's formula do not always go together – the pace is slow with lots of stops to take in the detail: coffee breaks amongst the alpine flowers; packed lunches surrounded by basalt columns and fossil oysters; time to discover an otter's track or an unusual lichen ... and always a pair of binoculars at hand, to spot the basking shark or an occasional minke whale.

Skye has long been regarded as a special place for the birdwatcher, the geologist, the botanist and marine biologist. By taking time to 'stand and stare' you will discover for yourself this hidden side of Skye – one that complements the traditional image of seascapes and mountain views.

Using the Maps

Each map has been drawn to the largest possible scale to show the specific positions of animal signs and plant life as well as any geological and archaeological features.

When a feature is named on the map, it is referred to within the text by using bold type (eg. **fly agaric**) to allow for easy cross-reference. An explanation of the symbols used on the maps can be found in the Map Key. Note in particular the symbols used for marking gates and stiles.

Each route (except Skeabost Island, Loch Bay and Clach Oscar) has been marked by a line of dashes. Please note that this does not indicate a well-worn path. On some walks, the path will be obvious and well trodden, but *there will be sections where there is no clear path to follow.*

Site numbers represent sites of significant interest. A short description of each site is given opposite the map for quick and easy reference whilst on the move.

1. Rubha Hunish

Checklist

Distance	4.5 miles/7.3km
Approximate time	Could be done in 3 to 4 hours but best take a picnic and allow all day
Maps	1: 25 000 OS Explorer 408. 1:50 000 British Geological Survey, Sheet 90
Terrain	Level moorland and coastal paths, damp in places. The path down to the Hunish peninsula is a steep, rocky scramble in its upper section
Equipment and Books	Binoculars, hand lens, sea shore and bird identification guides
Special considerations	June for bird watching: July-August for minke whales
Footwear	Boots
Parking	Purpose-built car park at NG422742

There's something special about rounding the top of an island. There is a sense of adventure and danger in going around the edge of a land mass – the tip, the end point, the limit of your journey; like Cape Horn or the Cape of Good Hope – a sense of entering another world.

This is wild country but you have to earn it. The road turns back here but you go on, over rising moorland to reach the cliff edge, only to discover a hidden sill of dolerite through which you must make your steep descent. Towering above are the petrified columns of Meall Tuath whilst below waits the cliffs of Hunish with its thousand seabirds and sparkling rock pools.

What did you do today? We sat looking across Lub a'Sgiathain, possibly the most exciting place in Skye – and d'you know what? There wasn't a car in sight!

It was an early start in early April. The clocks had just changed to British Summer Time. A south-westerly Force 5 with thin altostratus meant we had one clear window-of-a-day. The wind and bright sun was a shock to the face after the darkness of winter.

In the past, the start of this walk would have been from the telephone kiosk, but now parking is much easier from the purpose-built car park. Janet had the use of a GPS navigation contraption that would tell us the exact grid reference wherever we stopped. I had studied all the relevant geology maps and texts and so we were ready for a full day – binoculars, hand-lens, camera, and packed lunch.

The new start meant heading out from the car park along the Shulista road and then turning left after the cattle grid to follow a line of posts conveniently sited over the moor.

I had become obsessed with finding the 'glacial striae' marked clearly on the geology map. These were the scratch marks left by the moving ice that flowed across Trotternish 11,000 years ago. Every patch of exposed rock was carefully examined. We had barely gone a quarter of a mile before we were ready for a coffee break.

The map showed that we should encounter the first marks at NG422748 in a direction pointing west-south-west. But the surface of the exposed dolerite sill was a crazy pavement with lines going everywhere. How do you separate the bedding plains, faults, and cooling cracks from the striae?

"Can't find the striae!" became the familiar cry, the first of which came as we sat sipping coffee and trying the ginger biscuits. But there were great views behind of Sròn Vourlin and Sgurr Mòr forming the northern edge of the Storr-Quiraing ridge. Just before an old turf wall I found some **'tree' lichen** growing amongst the heather. "*Cladonia arbuscula!*" I shouted, but of course nobody was listening.

Focusing on the ground helps relieve any tedium in crossing such a moorland. It wasn't long before we were spotting green grassy mounds where birds had perched. After a rock outcrop and a group of stone ruins we spotted a raised grassy mound to the right of the path (**site 1**) which was a regular lookout perch for crows, with numerous pellets scattered around the thimble-shaped bumps. The grey wool-laden droppings indicated that this was also a territorial marking site for the local foxes.

After a brief descent, the path crossed more lines of turf walls. There were good views from here across the abandoned crofts of Erisco with Tulm Island and Duntulm Castle in the distance. Could

Tulm Island be a giant *roche moutonnée* sculpted by the moving ice? And where are these glacial striae?

We walked on through a gate in a new fence, taking care to bare left across some wooden planks crossing a wet hollow before regaining the path on drier land. We made good headway through the heather in a gentle climb. Somewhere along here was the second location of the glacial striae at NG414755.

From now on the excitement slowly increased ... The first skylarks, the first wheatears, a pair of ravens doing aerobatics above the edge of the dyke to our left. Two people standing in silhouette on the cliff edge between the two dykes. Keep moving. High expectation as we near the top of the rise. And then, suddenly, the coastguard station rears up in front with someone inside, peering out at us through the window! This is no longer used for wartime duty but is kept in good repair as a bothy for those wishing to spend a night in the wilds.

We walked to the cliff edge to see exactly why a coastguard station was built here (**site 2**). The view was spectacular, looking down the

Approaching the northern tip of Hunish (site 4) with its giant bubbles of thrift

Looking back towards the cliffs of Meall Tuath from the east side of Hunish

150 feet to the Hunish peninsula; like being in an aeroplane. What more could you want? The island of Trodday across to the right; Fladda-chùain and Lord MacDonald's Table to the left; a coastline that you have never seen before in any photograph of Skye that you know, and, Good Heavens! Is that really a sea stack?

Time for lunch. An idyllic spot out of the wind was what we wanted. We followed the path away from the coastguard station, cutting down through the first dyke of Meall Tuath (or could that be Minas Tirith?) and after skirting along past a sheep shelter and a brush with near-death in pondering how to get down onto the peninsula below, we had lunch on the gentle grass slope in an idyllic spot out of the wind under the second dyke.

Time to ponder the nature of the wetland between the two dykes. By carefully looking at its surface, you can just make out a herringbone pattern of drainage ditches, now abandoned, leaving the area to be reclaimed by the rising bog.

How to get down onto Hunish? It's not easy. There are no tracks marked on the OS maps. The hard bit is finding the start of the path. Don't, whatever you do, try and follow a gully that leads down from the edge of the first dyke, with its interesting wind-shaped *Ramalina siliquosa* lichen on the vertical wall, tempting you further ahead... Instead, look for a large broad boulder lying flat near the cliff edge, in front of the *second* (western-most) dyke. A narrow path leads past the west side of this boulder and then becomes a rocky staircase. The path is well worn and polished in places. It takes you down to a level section with a prominent sentinel-of-a-rock on the left and the remains of an improvised sheep shelter on the right. Notice the circular colony of white lichen with rust coming out from its base. Notice the roseroot.

The situation you are in is made more spectacular by the looming face of the dolerite sill above (**site 3**). Here can be found continuous vertical columns reaching 150 feet high. That's fifty feet higher than those found on the Kilt Rock. The extreme height of this dolerite sill allows for variations in form. This cliff has been extensively analysed into three zones. The bottom 40 feet is olivine dolerite which gives the surface a ropy bark-like texture. The next 120 feet is picrodolerite, a dense rock rich in magnesium and iron. The top 140 feet is less dense and lacks olivine but has a higher calcium content. It is this palette of chemicals that has produced the spectacular prismatic jointing reminiscent of Fingal's Cave and the Giant's Causeway.

The path becomes less steep with evidence of being built-up with a terrace along the bottom section. Now you reach the wind-blasted grass of Hunish with its run-rig and mounds of glacial debris. We followed a sheep track parallel to the west shore, passed the scattering of pools on our right and gullies on the left, to reach the northern tip of the peninsula (**site 4**). Here, on a grassy platform grow giant 'bubbles' of thrift: thrift like you have never seen before; not the flat meadows of pink flowers that you find on the road to Moll at the head of Loch Ainort; not the discrete basin-shaped mounds that you find above Dunvegan's Coral Beach. These are elephantine sculptures that have been deformed by wind and encouraged by salt spray and bird lime.

Here, on this northern-most tip you will see all the seabirds you could wish. The rocky island just below where you are sitting is a favourite site for shag and the occasional cormorant. Beyond is a major flight corridor for gannets, fulmar, guillemot, razorbill and kittiwake.

We continued towards the east side, passing a sharp gully and its adjacent dyke. Above the tide line, bright red iron oxide was weeping out from the junction of rocks. The short grass was dotted with stunted heather and the salt-tolerant crowberry. The occasional empty limpet shell with notches around its front end indicated the recent attention of an oystercatcher.

Now we reached the east side, higher than the west side, with cliffs tailor-made for guillemots, razorbills and kittiwakes. A dramatic rock

Fan-jointing in the dolerite sill overlooking the Bay of the Wing

bridge (**site 5**) leads across a gully with shags on either side, already sitting noisily on their nests. The grass on the cliff top had the now-familiar camel humps of thrift.

From here we had our first view of the sea stack, which we first spied from above. Then onwards, past a second stack, festooned with abandoned climbing slings and then further, a grass shelf led down to a shore of wondrous complexity, of bare rock dykes and gullies that funnel the waves only to have them explode into piles of pebbles the size of cannonballs. This is **site 6** although it could easily be sites 7, 8 or 9! Where to begin?

First, there is a lens of ostracod limestone trapped in the dolerite sill exposed above low water. It is a piece of the bed of limestone that lies in a band from Duntulm to Kilmaluag Bay. A single piece has been brought here by the molten lava, like a brazil nut trapped inside a bar of Thornton's toffee.

Next, the otter track that leads out from here, across the grass, halts at a patch of darker grass made dark from all the nitrogen from all the spraints regularly deposited here before continuing across to the next pebbly beach.

This is a good place to have a picnic. You need time here to appreciate the rock pools. They are some of the finest in Skye, which means they are some of the finest in the British Isles. One giant pool is formed by a fault line alongside a dyke. This is where the *Collins Pocket Guide to the Sea Shore* earns its keep. Thong weed, *Alectoria*, pepper dulse, ordinary dulse, carrageen, channel wrack, knotted wrack, saw wrack, and flat wrack; rough, smooth, edible and flat periwinkles; anemones that you never thought existed outside children's books; barnacles and limpets, but not as you known them. Take out the hand-lens; hands and knees; focus, and there they are – tiny black pits covering their surface, like pepper. What is it? *Arthopyrenia halodytes*. What more could a lichenologist ask for!

And then, as the shadows crept slowly across, I suddenly remembered that this was the site for a bed of concretionary sandstone as marked on the geological map. We scrambled to the side of a yellow-coloured cliff above the shore. And there it was: soft sandstone with nodules covered in fool's gold, and cross-bedding showing the ancient water currents of a shallow estuary that formed over 150 million years ago.

We were about to set back when Janet pointed to the cliff on the far side of the bay, now caught in the red light of the low sun. "Looks

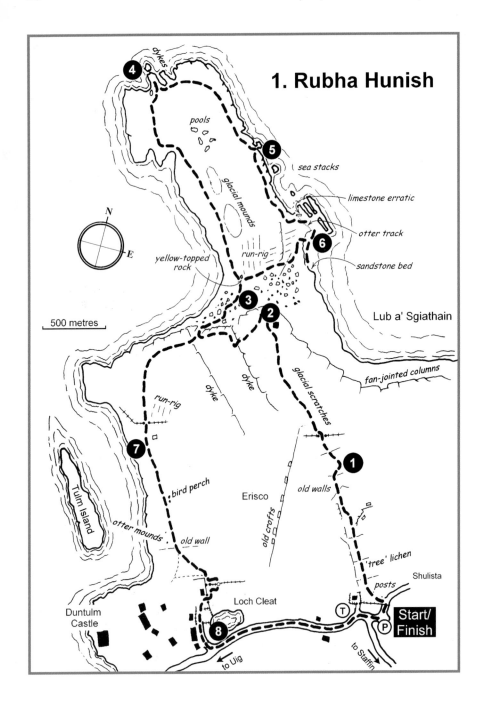

1. Rubha Hunish

Sites of Interest

1. Grass mounds (NG415754)
Lookout perches for hooded crows and territorial marking site for local foxes

2. Coastguard station (NG412762)
Cliff-top viewpoint looking north-west to Lord Macdonald's Table and north-east to Trodday

3. Basalt columns (NG411762)
150ft-high prismatic columns with hexagonal jointing

4. Hunish viewpoint (NG407768)
Northern-most tip of Skye. Major flight corridor for seabirds and feeding routes of minke whales and basking sharks

5. Rock bridge (NG411766)
Dolerite cliff with nesting shag, fulmar and kittiwake

6. Bay of the Wing (NG414764)
Rock pools, sea stacks and fossil beds, with views of fan-jointed basalt in the shape of a bird's wing

7. Dolerite sill (NG411753)
Views over Duntulm Bay with otter sprainting mounds on grassy foreshore

8. Loch Cleat (NG415741)
Freshwater loch with diatomite deposits. Whooper swans in winter and early spring

like a fan!" she said, and I remembered what this bay was all about. This was *Lùb a' Sgiathain*, which is Gaelic for 'Bay of the Wing'. There, lit up at the top of the 300ft cliff was a giant bird's wing carved in stone. It was a section of columnar dolerite that had been put under pressure from the side or had been influenced by some existing fault lines – whatever – no one is sure – but here it was: fan-jointing on a grand scale. Spectacular!

Now it was time to head back. We reached the path at the bottom of the climb at a **yellow-topped stone**, not just a convenient marker, but a regular perch for wheatears and pipits. At the top of the climb we followed the wet peaty track which led us down across the heather moor.

After a gate we followed the sunlit shore above Duntulm Bay (**site 7**). The dolerite sill was aligned horizontally and its surface was being eroded into tiny holes as though 'pecked and dressed' ready for building. The path passed yet more green mounds, that were used by birds, and some that were much larger with otter spraints on their tops.

The path cut across to a well-made wall, which it followed to a gate, but we crossed the fence 30 metres to the left of the gate at a delicate stile, before returning to follow the wall. The path turned right through a second gate and took us on past the coastguard cottages and Loch Cleat (**site 8**). On this April evening, six whooper swans were waiting to greet us with their characteristic trumpet calls: a fitting end to a memorable day!

2. Quiraing

Checklist

Distance	4.5 miles/7.3km
Approximate time	3.5 to 4 hours
Maps	1: 25 000 OS Explorer 408. 1:50 000 British Geological Survey, Sheet 90
Terrain	Mostly well worn paths with two rocky sections around gullies
Footwear	Boots
Parking	Parking area at road summit (NG439679)

Everyone knows the Quiraing. It's one of those iconic national landscapes like the butts and mesas of North America or the eroded limestone hills of China. Enough years had gone by without having walked it. And so when Mike, Cathy and John were here for my 'sixtieth', we had to do it. They even brought a bottle of champagne to celebrate with the idea of opening it on 'The Table'.

We parked the car in the one remaining space at the top of the Staffin-Uig road. It was Saturday and busy, even though it was blowing a Force 5 with light rain and drizzle. And so, with over-trousers on from the start and my new digital voice recorder in hand, we set off to monitor the event.

There was a holiday atmosphere with minibuses decanting every nationality and everyone enjoying the mountain experience. We took our place in the line of hooded wanderers, following the well-worn but narrow track towards a view that I had seen so many times in guide books, and in adverts for posh cars.

Then it was over a culvert hiding a lush patch of **hard fern**. All along the sides of the path there were alpine flowers, especially Alpine lady's mantle. Moss campion grew at eye level on the left.

Sites of Interest

1. **Rocky gully (NG441681)**
   Water-worn basalt with alpine flowers

2. **Sheltered dell (NG451686)**
   Fertile hollows amongst boulders below The Prison with
   opposite-leaved golden saxifrage

3. **Lochan (NG451696)**
   Water horsetail and reflections of the Quiraing

4. **Stile (NG449703)**
   Views north across Meall Tuath to Harris

5. **Summit (NG449693)**
   Cairn on ridge with view of The Table

We reached the first of two tricky gullies (**site 1**). Everyone seemed to have these new-fangled walking poles that would appear to be of some value yet needed to be carried for most of these sections. Maybe I'm living on a different planet, but if I was going to carry something around all day like that, I'd want it to at least double-up as an umbrella, or have a flask of brandy concealed in the handle. And what's wrong with an ordinary walking stick anyway? Do we really need a carbon-fibre fully-extending pole with ergonomically-designed shock-absorbing handles? But then, I've reached a 'grumpy sixty', and the world has changed.

The views were as stunning as the magazine photos, and the mist only added to the atmosphere. In front was the bulky mass of **The Prison**, a block of basalt that had slipped down sometime in the Pleistocene. This incredible landscape is even more amazing when you uncover its anatomy. Basalt lava is resting on top of sandstones and shales, which in turn are sat on top of a dolerite sill. Imagine a pack of dominoes standing upright (the basalt). They are resting on a beer mat (the shale) on top of a highly polished bar table (the dolerite). Someone knocks the table just enough to cause some of the dominoes to lean backwards and slide away from the remaining pack.

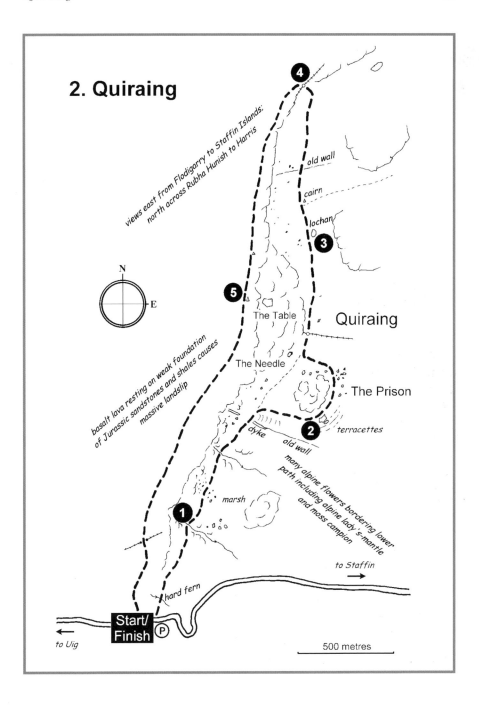

2. Quiraing

views east from Flodigarry to Staffin Islands;
north across Rubha Hunish to Harris

old wall

cairn

lochan

3

N
E

5

The Table

Quiraing

The Needle

basalt lava resting on weak foundation
of Jurassic sandstones and shales causes
massive landslip

The Prison

2

terracettes

dyke   old wall

many alpine flowers bordering lower
path including alpine lady's-mantle
and moss campion

1

marsh

to Staffin

hard fern

Start/
Finish   P

to Uig

500 metres

If you catch the movement just right, the profile of collapsed dominoes matches the profile of the Quiraing.

We turned off the main path to skirt round The Prison. The path dropped into a lush dell of opposite-leaved golden saxifrage (**site 2**) before climbing gently around the eastern ramparts. For the first time we escaped the wind and found a sheltered spot to have lunch. Coffee and biscuits and a quick look at the lichens and a photograph of **The Needle** rising out of the mist. We moved on, up a steep grassy slope to reach the upper path which took us over a fence and then past a miniature Kilnsey Crag with sudden views of the northern ridge and the islands beyond. The walk led through a quiet landscape of **mossy boulders** and hummocks with a curtain-wall of sheer basalt ever present on our left.

We reached a small lochan filled with water horsetail (**site 3**). The

Path from The Prison leading north below The Needle

On reaching the main Quiraing ridge (site 4) with the view north over Meall Tuath to Fladda-chùain and Harris

reflected silhouettes of the basalt ridge appeared on the smooth surface like 'Rorschach Inkblots'. Total silence. No wind, just mist.

The narrow path snaked its way up to the skyline and crossed a stile onto the ridge (**site 4**). We were still below the base of the stratus and could see the twin dykes of Meal Tuath standing guard over the descent into Hunish. We turned left and began our ascent of the Quiraing main ridge.

The views over Flodigarry and Staffin were special with their respective islands playing hide-and-seek amongst the landslip. But we were heading into the wind and were soon above the cloud base. Drizzle turned to rain. A cairn appeared (**site 5**). Was this the top? Was this the marker to mark the spectacular view straight down onto **The**

Table? We were getting wetter and the fun was over. On a fine day this would be one of the best viewpoints anywhere in Britain.

We followed the grassy path, which became muddier and steeper as we approached the car park. It was late afternoon when we arrived back at the car. Just one other vehicle alongside ours had a group of hardy souls returning from Holland. I was obviously suffering from exposure at this point (witness the disintegrating syntax). Mike had completely lost it, having a conversation with a Dutch driver for five minutes before realising it wasn't me.

3. The Storr

Checklist

Distance	4.3 miles/7.0km
Approximate time	4 hours
Maps	1: 25 000 OS Explorer 408. 1:50 000 British Geological Survey, Sheet 80E & Part of 81
Terrain	Faint grassy path followed by rocky bealach to reach ridge. Summit ridge dry with short grass. Rocky decent (tricky in icy conditions) followed by easy well-made path through woods
Footwear	Boots
Parking	Car park at side of the A855 north of Loch Leathan (NG509529)

You won't believe this, but I have lived on Skye for over 30 years and have never been to the top of the Storr. I had once visited the Old Man sometime in the early 70s but then the path was just a muddy scramble through a plantation that had only just been planted. And so, as it was perfect weather and our son was staying with us over New Year, and as there was nothing I could do in the garden, there was absolutely no excuse.

It was the day after New Year's Day, 2009. I specify the date because it was one of the best winter days in Skye for the past ten years. The ground was rock-solid, hoar frost was everywhere, and the views were at their theoretical limit, only halted by the curvature of the Earth. No wind, brilliant sunshine and hardly a soul to be seen *anywhere.*

We packed the rucksacks, collected our neighbour, who hadn't been on the Storr either, and set off to Portree. The drive along the

Staffin road was full of expectation. Another mile and we were approaching Loch Fada. At 9am, the foreground was still in shadow and the Old Man was just beginning to catch the sun.

We stopped at the car park, now much improved. One family in a camper van was just finishing breakfast, otherwise not a soul. Boots on, and off we go heading south, away from the traditional direction. We were going to save the best until last.

We followed the road and then cut across to the right towards the ridge at Bealach Beag. It was one of those days when you are glad to have a digital camera with a one-gigabyte memory card. The sun was glinting off the icy road all the way into Portree and beyond. Click. Loch Leathan with its side road was like white icing sugar. Ben Tianavaig could be seen for what it was – an extension of the east coast landslip. Dun Caan on Raasay was so clear you could actually make out the pale lava flow sloping down from its flat top. Click.

We approached the foot of the climb up the stony gully of the bealach. Time for a break and a cup of coffee and biscuits. To the south, we could see the Lochan a'Bhealaich Bhig with its overgrown

View from the summit of the Storr looking south towards the Cuillin

scree slopes. To the north was a tantalising glimpse of the shattered pinnacles of the Storr. The sun was low and highlighted every sheep track criss-crossing the flat ground below.

The horizontal lava flows could be clearly seen, but one spot was glinting bright red as the sunlight caught a freshly eroded layer. As we climbed we passed Alpine lady's mantle, thyme and mossy saxifrage, all just leaves and mere apologies of what they would become later in the year (**site 1**).

At last we reached the ridge. John was way ahead and shouts back something about taking some photos. He had forgotten his camera. Normally the potential to take 300 photos would lessen the stress, but now I realised just how special these conditions were and the pressure was on.

There are those who enjoy a walk for the moment, and there are those who spoil the moment by trying to capture it forever on camera. And here I was, trying to capture it forever! Tension. Have I the right lens? Damn! Forgot to bring the standard lens and only have the 200mm zoom. But who wants to be cluttered with all that extra equipment and be forever changing lenses? Just relax and enjoy the moment.

Torridon. You can see every gully on Ben Alligin. I swear we could have seen the street lamps outside the village hall if we could have seen around the corner. Glad I've got the telephoto.

We followed the ridge where you overlook the Sanctuary and for the first time we get a close-up view of the Old Man (**site 2**). Beyond is Ullapool, Stac Polly, Suilvan and Ben Hope.

We passed a strange surface pattern in a group of boulders (**site 3**). This iron-rich rock is called 'mugearite', and the star-like grooves on its surface are where feldspar crystals have been eroded away. Wish I'd brought the standard lens. But then, there was that amazing view over Portree – getting better as we climbed higher.

We climbed the gentle slope around the rim of Coire Faoin. Two ravens landed on the edge before taking flight again. A glance at the geology memoir showed we were walking over frost shattered 'regolyth' – ground that had been left exposed above the ice sheet that had surrounded the Storr ridge 11,000 years ago. Back then, the exposed islands of basalt were repeatedly frozen and thawed, shattering the surface to leave matchbox-sized rock fragments covering the summit (**site 4**).

Now the whole ridge to the north came into view, from Hartaval,

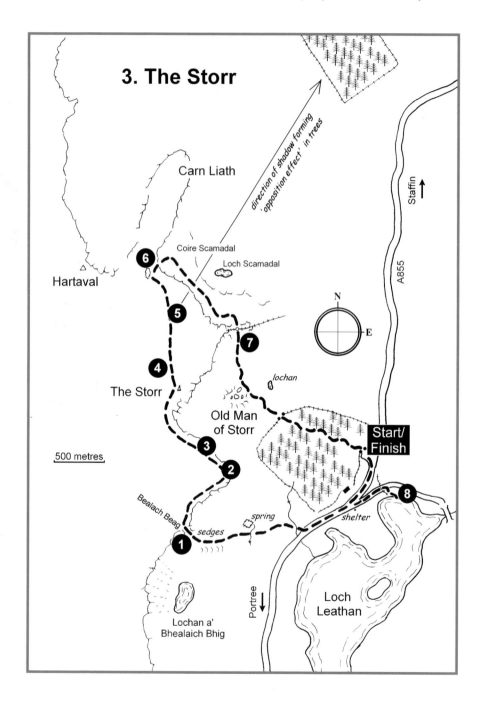

3. The Storr

Carn Liath

direction of shadow forming 'opposition effect' in trees

Hartaval

Coire Scamadal

Loch Scamadal

Staffin

A855

6

5

N

E

4

The Storr

lochan

Old Man of Storr

7

500 metres

3

2

Start/Finish

Bealach Beag

spring

sedges

shelter

8

1

Portree

Lochan a' Bhealaich Bhig

Loch Leathan

Sites of Interest

1. Rocky gorge (NG493530)
Eroding basalt supporting a rich variety of alpine plants including mossy saxifrage and Alpine lady's mantle

2. Viewpoint (NG496535)
Overlooking The Sanctuary and the Old Man with the Scottish mainland to the north-east

3. Eroded rock patterns (NG495536)
Unusual star patterns in exposed outcrops of 'mugearite' lava

4. Storr 'nunatak' (NG495540)
Frost-weathered rocks above 600 metres, suggests the summit peaks of the ridge were left exposed to frost action above the ice sheet during the last Ice Age

5. View of 'opposition effect' (NG494545)
The low winter sun casts shadows onto conifer plantation 2.5 miles to the north east. Each person sees a bright patch in the foliage where their own shadow would be formed

6. Frost-shattered tor (NG494551)
Evidence of frost action above the trimline of the last ice sheet that covered the lower slopes 11 000 years ago

7. Viewpoint (NG501545)
Reverse view of the Old Man of Storr in silhouette

8. Musical sand (NG508526)
After being washed by rain and then dried in the sun, the quartz grains along this northern shore may produce 'squeaking sounds' when walked upon

Beinn Edra and on to the Quiraing with the islands of Fladdha a' chùain beyond. The view west was equally spectacular with Loch Bracadale and Macleod's Tables, with Roneval on Harris and Eaval on Uist on the far horizon.

The summit of the Storr was an arctic scene that day. There had to be more photos with someone sitting down in the foreground – a bit further left please, to make a silhouette. The Cuillin made up the back drop. Perfect!

Now it was time to head down, heading north, parallel with the ridge. At two o'clock in the afternoon we were in shadow and it was cold, probably minus 5. We found the sun on our backs as we reached the edge of the escarpment (**site 5**). Those familiar with this walk will know that the view north-east towards Staffin is interrupted in the mid-foreground by the extensive conifer plantation of Tote Forest. The sun was casting our shadows in the direction of the trees. They were too far away for us to see our own shadows on the foliage but conditions were right to provide an unusual optical phenomenon known as 'the opposition effect'.

Late afternoon sun behind the observer creates a bright patch amongst the trees in Tote Forest caused by the 'oppostion effect'

Our shadows were being formed three miles away below us at what is called the antisolar point – exactly the same distance below the horizon that the sun is above it. In such conditions, the light reflects back brightly from surfaces that have a rough texture, reflecting directly back towards the sun and so back into your eyes. The light that returns from surrounding areas of the plantation to the side of the antisolar point is not as bright, because it is picking out shadows. The result is a brightly-lit patch of conifer that moves along with you as you move.

We needed to find some shelter from the wind and have lunch. We chose an isolated outcrop of basalt described in the geological memoir as a 'frost-shattered tor' (**site 6**). We were still above the 500 metre-high 'trimline' marking the limit of the last ice sheet. To the left, below the trimline, in the col leading to Hartaval, were a group of *roches moutonnée*, their shape indicating that the ice had moved through the bealach in a north-easterly direction.

Now we needed to retreat, back to the car park. We cut through the ridge at a low point and descended to the path that skirts well above **Loch Scamadal**. This section had been in shadow all day and the icy path was tricky in parts.

We crossed a fence where a convenient stone had been placed for a stile. We were still in shadow when suddenly the Old Man and his companions appeared in silhouette. There was still some room left on the memory card.

Some children were playing on the frozen **lochan** below. There are some sounds that stay with you. They are like nothing else. The sound of bits of ice being skimmed across a frozen loch and that eerie resonance that seems to echo across the drum-like surface ...

We joined the main path through the forest plantation. Suddenly, all was quiet. It was like entering a room with thick carpets and curtains as we dropped down to the car park from where we had started.

Postscript

As there was still some daylight left, we decided to check out one of Skye's least-known sites. Loch Leathan is the only place in Skye where you can find 'musical sands'. The classic site is on Eigg at the Bay of Laig, initially described by Hugh Millar in *The Cruise of the Betsey*. Such musical sands are rare. They squeak or boom depending on their grain size and shape.

Skimming ice on the frozen lochan below the Old Man of Storr

We walked along the roadside path to the bus shelter, crossed the **cattle grid** and then cut down to the loch in eager expectation (**site 8**). It looked promising. We could see the shore had been formed of fine sand with different strandlines with different grades of sand that had been sorted by wave and wind action. The prevailing winds are from the south east and so the whole reach of the loch can generate a substantial wave action which deposits material along this northern shore.

"It's supposed to sing when you kick it," I said. But of course it did nothing of the kind. It was frozen solid and was keeping stum.

Apparently, to get the best sounds, it needs to be perfectly dry after being thoroughly washed after a period of rain. I broke the surface with the heel of my boot and collected a small sample in a plastic bag.

When we got home, I dried it on a tray by the fire. The next day I poked it. Nothing – except, possibly the suggestion of a brittle squeak. But I had made a grave methodological error. By taking a mixture of grains from across the shore, I had not accounted for the effect of 'sorting'. The different strandlines had grains that had been sorted into different sizes. I had broken through them without thinking that the sound may depend on grains resonating with others of the same size.

Notes

Hugh Millar's references to musical sand can be found in *The Cruise of the Betsey*, W P Nimmo, 1873, pp. 58-67.

Loch Leathan is described as a site of 'musical sand' by Anderson and Dunham, *The Geology of Northern Skye*, HMSO 1966, pp.34 and 196.

A recent study of the Ice Age and its effects on the Trotternish ridge can be found in *The Quaternary of the Isle of Skye: Field Guide*, C K Ballantyne *et al.*, Quaternary Research Association, 1991. pp14-16.

The Old Man of Storr was first climbed via a route on the north side in 1955 by a party led by Don Whillans. A route up the south side was climbed in 1967 by Lee and Thomson. Don't even think about it!

4. Scorrybreac

Checklist

Distance	1.86 miles/3km
Approximate time	1.5 to 2 hours
Maps	1: 25 000 OS Explorer 409 or 410. 1:50 000 British Geological Survey, Sheet 80E and Part of 81
Terrain	Well-maintained footpaths
Footwear	Boots
Parking	Follow the A855 Staffin road out of Portree and take the right-hand turn off to Budmhor and the Cuillin Hills Hotel. There is a parking space marked for 4 cars at the road end (NG488438)

When you want to escape the crowds of Portree and you have a few hours to spare, this is the perfect place to visit. There are wildflowers and lichens and lots of Latin names, and always the chance of a seal or a sea eagle. Easy paths, easy to follow, all on Portree's doorstep – surely something this good should require more effort!

From the car park, a tarmac path leads to a boathouse and **slipway** and then continues as a gravel path through a tunnel of hazel. The route has been maintained by the Clan Nicolson and all along this first section are **memorial stones** and seats in honour of clan members.

This south-facing side of the bay is sheltered and there are extensive growths of dog rose and occasional large specimens of goat willow amongst the hazel. The footpath has patches of **red stones** from the top layer of a basalt lava flow. This is characteristic of basalt where there has been long time periods between outpourings, allowing time for iron in the surface rocks to oxidize.

The coastline turns the corner at the rocky outcrop of **Sgeir Mhòr**, or 'Black Rock' (**site 1**). This is a dolerite sill. The rock itself is not black but appears black because of the marine lichens that cover its surface. The footpath along this section is bordered by a surprising variety of wildflowers. During the summer months you will find clusters of the northern marsh orchid – deep purple flowers on stalks up to nine inches high. Late summer produces swathes of knapweed and scabious.

To the left of the path is a memorial **spring** enclosed by a framework of stone. On some occasions, after a prolonged spell of wet and misty weather, I have found otter spraints here.

Just past the spring, a dolerite **dyke** runs down to the path from the left with fine growths of bell heather and wood sage. The path now drops down through tall bracken with a patch of eared willow on

The start of the walk overlooking Portree Bay

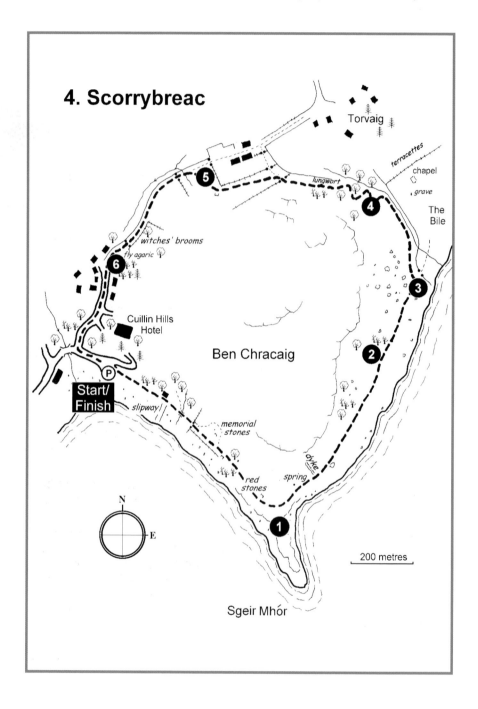

4. Scorrybreac

Torvaig

terracettes

chapel

grave

The Bile

lungwort

witches' brooms

fly agaric

Cuillin Hills Hotel

Ben Chracaig

Start/Finish

slipway

memorial stones

red stones

spring

dyke

N

E

Sgeir Mhór

200 metres

Sites of Interest

1. **'Black Rock' (NG494435)**
   Dolerite sill with shoreline covered in black lichen. Cormorants drying their wings. Path-side flowers include orchids, knapweed and scabious

2. **Aspen grove (NG49543)**
   Silver-grey bark and leaves that tremble on long, flattened stems. Rosettes of lead-coloured lichen on older trunks

3. **Wall and gate (NG496440)**
   View of fertile fields above Jurassic cliffs. Effects of iron stains produced by lichens on wall and surrounding boulders

4. **Zig-zag path (NG495443)**
   View of Bile Chapel and solitary grave. Terracettes on landslipped-slopes

5. **Boggy section (NG491445)**
   Yellow flowers of bog asphodel, the 'bone breaker', growing in peat soil

6. **Ash tree (NG488441)**
   'Old-forest-indicator lichens' including *Sticta* smelling of fish

the right. The basalt cliffs tower above you on the left and it is here in a cave 400 feet above the shoreline that a local robber, MacCoiter, once had his lookout and kept his stolen goods.

Keep a careful watch on the left of the path for a group of tall trees with silvery-grey bark (**site 2**). These are aspen and it is likely that they all share identical DNA having spread from an original parent plant. Stop and listen. Even in the slightest breeze, the aspen leaves shimmer and rustle due to their long flattened leaf stalks – hence its Latin name *Populus tremula*. The rosettes of lichen on the bark look as though they have been carved out of lead and have the Latin name *Degelia plumbea*.

After a narrow undulating section, you reach a wall and a gate (**site**

Approaching the gate overlooking the Beal (site 3)

3). There are excellent views right, over the bay to Ben Tianavaig and Dùn Caan on Raasay. The gently-sloping fields on the other side of the wall is an area known as the **The Bile** (pronounced 'Beal'). The rock below the surface is fossil-bearing Jurassic which is rich in calcium minerals. The effect shows in the grass which appears a brighter green than the grasses and sedges on the basalt.

Notice the stone on the top of the wall to the right of the gate. The pale grey lichen is surrounded by a brown-red stain – iron oxide that is being dissolved from the basalt by various acids produced by the lichen. The stained surface is bare of growth. On vertical surfaces the oxides accumulate along the bottom margin of the lichen colony and eat into the once-circular edge.

Sailor's grave outside Beal Chapel

Don't go through the gate but turn left to follow the narrow path, keeping the wall on your right. In summer, look for creamy-pink flowers of scented orchid. You pass several red fuschia bushes and then the path turns and climbs left up a series of zig-zags through tall bracken, rowan, birch and hazel with lady's mantle on the path sides.

Once you have gained some height (**site 4**), look back for a view over the top of The Bile. At the top of the field are the ruins of a Celtic **chapel**, hidden amongst a tall stand of nettles. It is marked by a large alder tree at its north end. Below the chapel is a solitary **grave** where the coxswain of HMS Porcupine was buried in 1861.

Above the flat field, there are steep grass slopes covering landslipped material at the base of the basalt. They show the characteristic pattern of **terracettes** which often develops on sheep-grazed slopes of 45 degrees.

At the top of the zig-zag climb, the path levels out. Notice two old trees on the right, in front of an old wall. They are covered in **lungwort** lichen (*Lobaria pulmonaria*). The path now follows the old wall. Notice the top of the wall covered in moss (*Rhacomitrium lanuginosum*). When dry it appears hoary and grey like 'frizzy hair'. It only colonizes horizontal surfaces.

The path drops steadily and after a kissing gate, forks left over an area of grass and *Calluna* heather. At a wooden bench there is a sudden view of the Old Man of Storr. The narrow path drops down to a post with a waymark arrow. Just before reaching the post, you cross a boggy section (**site 5**) with bog asphodel on the path side. The Latin name *Narthecium ossifragum*, reflects a belief once held – that if eaten by livestock, it would beak their bones. The plant grows in acid bogs where calcium levels are low.

Turn left at the waymark and follow the path across an open area before entering woodland. Where the path follows a wire fence on the left, notice a birch with what looks like a bird's nest in its branches. These clumps of twigs are known as **'witches' brooms'** and are characteristic of birch growing in damp surrounding. It is caused by the fungus *Taphrina betulina*.

The next gate leads into a mature section of birchwood. From late August the ground below these trees supports a variety of fungi including the poisonous **fly agaric**. The path now drops steadily passing an area of larch with beard like growths of *Usnea* lichen, and then, just before reaching the tarmac road, an ash tree takes you completely by surprise. Here, just left of the path is a tree covered in wonderful things (**site 6**). One metre up grows lungwort – apple green on top, pale cream underneath. Alongside is *Sticta fuliginosa* – a real stinker, which on a wet day smells of fish. A little higher and you find *Degelia* 'of-the-leaden-look', and then a whole mosaic of crustose lichens leaving not an inch of bark uncovered.

The path leads down to the road which takes you back to the starting point.

5. Skeabost Island

Checklist

Distance	0.4 miles/0.6km
Approximate time	15 minutes and upwards
Maps	1: 25 000 OS Explorer 410
Terrain	Gravel approach path; tussocky grass once on island
Special considerations	This site is a Scheduled Ancient Monument. It is a an offence to damage or deface any of the structures or stones
Footwear	In dry weather, shoes are adequate
Parking	Space for several cars along side of 'old road' east of Skeabost Bridge (NG420485)

The fast road past Skeabost takes you over the River Snizort. Hardly anyone stops. Must get on. Have to reach Portree. And so you miss the island: an oasis of calm; a gem of a place, hidden away from the busy world.

St Columba's Island is a wonderful archaeological site in its own right. Its church is sometimes referred to as the 'Cathedral of the Isles'. It is said that 28 clan chiefs are buried in the small chapel at the north-west end.

The first record of this being a religious site comes from 11th-century Norwegian documents associated with the Archdiocese of Trondheim. The cathedral building was thought to have been built sometime in the early 1300s but after the Reformation in the 16th Century the structure began to fall into decline.

From the main Portree road, take the side road to Prabost and cut off left past the Skeabost Memorial Hall. Just before the Skeabost Bridge, a gravel path leads you along the north bank of the River Snizort.

Look closely at the water. It will invariably have a pattern on its surface; like the waxed endpapers of an old book; like the fractals in a Benoit Mandelbrot set; self repeating sequences, swirl upon swirl.

Most Highland rivers carry natural 'surfactants' – soap-like compounds derived from plants growing on the peat moor – which may lead to the formation of bubbles and foam along turbulent sections. The section below the bridge frequently displays these complex patterns (**site 1**).

Follow the path to where it crosses a footbridge. Notice the fine lichens on the birch and elder on the right. The bridge spans a small island hidden by the foliage, before reaching the main island.

This is a special place out of reach of grazing sheep and cattle. The grass is occasionally strimmed around the gravestones. This means that taller herbs such as knapweed, wood avens and water avens can grow and set seed. In the boggy sections around the perimeter, look for the dark red flowers of marsh cinquefoil

Scattered around the island are groups of elder which were sometimes planted on sacred sites. This is a place to wander, discovering the ancient grave slabs amongst the more recent memorials and gravestones. The tallest building (**site 2**), is believed

left: Fractal patterns in river
below Skeabost Bridge
top: Plaque on the approach
to the island
above: Grave slab inside
the Chapel

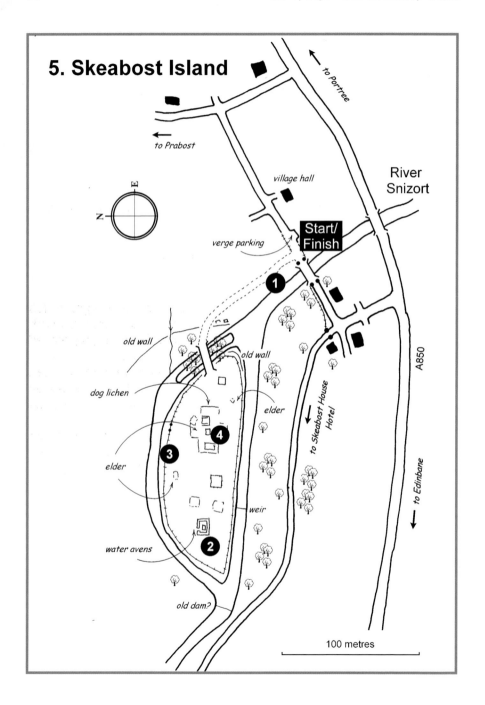

5. Skeabost Island

to Portree

to Prabost

River
Snizort

village hall

Start/
Finish

verge parking

N E

old wall

1

old wall

dog lichen

elder

elder

4

3

weir

water avens

2

old dam?

to Skeabost House Hotel

A850

to Edinbane

100 metres

Sites of Interest

1. River surface (NG419485)
Fractal patterns formed by natural surfactants from peat

2. Chapel (NG418485)
Medieval ruined chapel with grave slab depicting a knight holding a claymore

3. Wire fence (NG418485)
Growth of lichen restricted by run-off from top wire and staples

4. White grave slab (NG418485)
Old stone slab covered in white crustose lichens

to be early medieval rather than of Celtic origin. Inside is a grave slab of a knight holding a claymore. The surrounding walls are built with lime mortar which is being colonized by the lilac flowering ivy-leaved toadflax. Outside the entrance there are **water avens**.

The wire fence that surrounds the island shows how metals can affect lichens (**site 3**). Fine specimens of crottle and *Usnea* grow on the post tops but are being restricted immediately below the rusting iron wire and staples.

One of the grave slabs (**site 4**) has been left with its lichens intact and is almost completely covered in a white crust. The colonising lichen increases its diameter by about one millimetre each year – indicating the extreme age of these memorials.

6. Loch Bay ✓

Checklist

Distance	1.6 miles/2.5km
Approximate time	30 to 45 minutes
Maps	1: 25 000 OS Explorer 407. 1:50 000 British Geological Survey, Sheet 80W
Terrain	Pebble and rocky shore
Footwear	Boots
Parking	Turn off the A850 at Fairy Bridge and follow the single-track road to Stein village. There is a large car park at the road end, in front of the jetty (NG263563)

Some walks you plan in advance and have high expectations. Some walks just happen and are an unexpected delight. Who would have thought anything special about parking at the jetty at Stein and walking along the shore?

You won't find this mentioned in any walking guide. After all, who needs instructions on how to walk down a jetty and then pick your way along a pebbly shore? It's just a bit of beach isn't it? Somewhere to stretch the legs after driving to get here; perhaps take a quick photo of the sunset with that nice foreground of fishing boats, and then a quick look round the craft shops before a meal at the local pub or restaurant.

And yet, here is a walk to savour in its own right: Jurassic fossils everywhere; history from Telford to Boswell and Johnson; wild flowers and rock pools; no ropes or super fitness required – just sheer delight from start to finish!

We had arrived early at Stein. I can't remember whether it was our twenty-sixth or twenty-seventh wedding anniversary, or whether it was my sixtieth birthday, or if we had just come to have someone else cook the meal. The point is, we like celebrating here, but on this occasion we had arrived too early and we had half an hour to kill.

Thirty years in Skye and we had never walked along this beach. For the first time we found ourselves taking the short slipway to the left of the jetty.

You have to be here in the afternoon or evening. Mornings are no good for this side of Waternish. This particular 'wing' of Skye lights up after midday. That's when it catches the sun. That's when you see the sublime seascapes over Isay, Mingay and Clett with North Uist beyond and the shallow cone of Pabbay over the Sound of Harris, and Harris itself with the sun going down. There is no better sunset in the Hebrides.

Stein jetty

Come here on a June evening and it's still light at 11 o'clock. Come here in July and wait until dark. Throw a pebble in the water by the jetty (**site 1**). If there has been a north westerly wind for the past few days, there is a chance the sea will flash with green light as the stone cuts through the surface. Fill a glass jar with some of the water by the shore. If it flashes and flickers as you shake it, you have captured a marine alga, appropriately name: *Noctiluca scintillans*.

But it was April and the tide was out.

The low cliff to the south of the jetty is just an apology of a cliff by Skye standards. It is in fact the edge of a raised beach. The area behind, up to the road, was the original shore, now raised after the ice has gone, now filled with reeds. The exposed clay contains pebbles and glacial drift. It is slipping continuously onto the shore.

Today it was full of primroses. Amongst the stones at the top of the shore we found 'curled docks', with leaves much narrower than the usual docks found in the garden, and better-able to withstand the drying action of salt.

And then the first rocks appeared that said this shoreline was special. A block of fossil shells, bivalves, each the size of a fingernail, packed solid into a creamy white limestone block – *Neomiodon*, then another with larger shells called *Unio*, both bivalve molluscs (which means they have shells in two halves connected by an elastic ligament). Next a block of extinct oysters – *Praeexogyra hebridica* masses of shells, eroding away to expose the grey mud-filled body shape. All these rocks belong to what geologists call the Great Estuarine Group. They contain animals that lived in shallow estuaries and shore lagoons 150 million years ago.

The beds are exposed all around the margins of

***Neomiodon* fossils: part of the Great Estuarine Group indicating fresh water conditions**

Loch Bay. They are found on Mingay where a limekiln was once operated to make quicklime. Such is the historical importance of the Loch Bay deposits, there are records going back to 1786, of an open boat making the hazardous journey across from Harris with a mason on board, specifically to quarry limestone to take back to Harris.

About 100 metres from the new jetty, below a fenced-off ruin, there is a line of boulders disappearing into the sea (**site 2**). This is where Thomas Telford built the first pier at Stein. It was completed in 1798, using local dressed stone as an outer skin with smaller rocks as an infill. He used a revolutionary new cement called 'Parker's Cement' that had been invented by a Mr Parker of Lambeth a few years earlier. The cement (also known as Roman Cement) was able to set under water and was so effective that it was later used in the construction of the Caledonian Canal.

On ths April day, the cliff face above the top of the shore was full of primroses, and alongside a freshly-eroded section were the yellow dandelion-like flowers of **coltsfoot**. On the shore below was a large volcanic boulder full of angular chunks of broken limestone – what geologists call 'breccia'. The pebbly shore had silverweed at its top, still not in flower but showing its silver filigree leaves.

There were more primroses and more landslip before reaching a second ruin,

Fossil oysters indicate marine and brackish conditions

a cottar's cottage, just above the shore (**site 3**). The walls contained a number of limestone blocks with evidence that at least some of the material was taken from the shore. A prominent piece to the left of the main opening was riddled with holes caused by the piddock – a marine creature that is able to drill through rock using its shell as an auger. Some of the holes still contained remnants of its curved shell

The old boat at the top of the shore was notable for its covering of bright orange marine lichen colonizing its plastic deck. Below, in the exposed dolerite sill, we found the smooth surface of an embedded lens of limestone. A few metres further, a pavement of cracked and crazed shale was exposed showing signs of being heated and baked by contact with the volcanic sill.

At this point the shore was flanked by **reed beds** and a grass that looks like barley but wasn't. We passed a section at the base of the clay cliff showing rounded pebbles – more evidence of the raised beach.

The **oak keel** of a wrecked boat marked the spot where a stream entered the shore. We crossed the stream and approached three large boulders lower down the shore (**site 4**). Getting excited. Great lichens here: white circles of crab's eye lichen but no signs of iron stains below; grey-green straps of sea ivory; bright orange rosettes of *Caloplaca*; and a black layer covering everything else. Is this tar? Has there been an oil spill? No, this is the lichen *Verrucaria maura*. If you look closely at its surface with a hand lens, it looks like a verruca or wart. It forms the characteristic black zone above the grey-white barnacle zone that you see everywhere at low tide. And here's a barnacle, *Chthalamus stellatus,* and joy! – look at its surface, peppered with tiny black pits where the endolithic lichen, *Arthopyrenia halodytes,* has eaten into its surface …

About 150 metres further on, we noticed some strange marks on an exposed rock on the mid shore (**site 5**). Zig-zags, slightly paler than the rock surface. Hand-lens out. This is the first time I've seen this outside a textbook – the track of a foraging limpet that has grazed the alga from the surface of a limestone lenticle. The radula or tongue is like a moving conveyer belt with rasp-like teeth. The limpet sways from side to side and efficiently clears an area of algae before returning back to its home base.

The limestone is also covered in the green seaweed *Enteromorpha intestinalis*, delicious when fried with sesame oil – honestly. The first brown seaweeds at the top of the sill are the two-inch-long straps of channel wrack. The underside held against the rock has a narrow

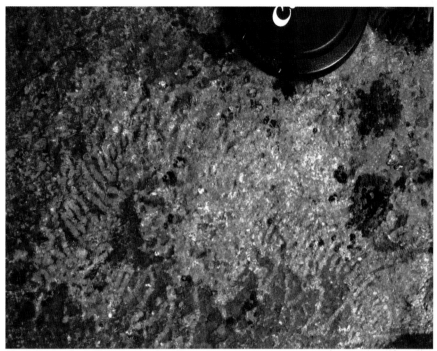

Radula marks left by a grazing limpet

channel which retains moisture when the tide goes out. Lower down the shore are long brown threads with bladders like knots - knotted wrack - indicating sheltered water.

We now passed slabs of modern **concrete** scattered haphazardly at the top of the shore. A pair of **oystercatchers** flew off from the rocks at low water. This is their territory and toward the end of May into late June, their nest will be hidden amongst the pebbles somewhere above the high tide strand line.

Thirty metres further and masses of oyster beds begin to appear on the shore. Some geologists assume these to have been washed up from a bed below sea level. We found fragmented sections breaking through the clay in a steep grass bank at the back of the shore (**site 6**). And then a surprise: a few metres further at the top of the shore were slabs of limestone with no shells. Their top surface was weathered and etched unlike any of the other rocks on the shore - a rare example of **nodular algal limestone.**

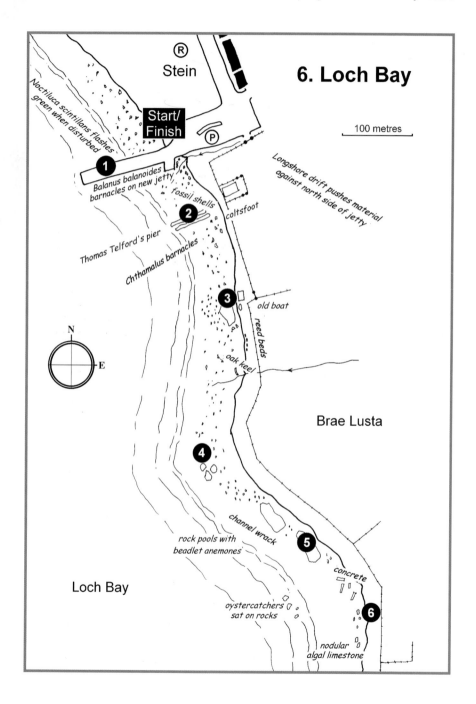

Noctiluca scintillans flashes green when disturbed

® Stein

Start/Finish

Ⓟ

6. Loch Bay

100 metres

Longshore drift pushes material against north side of jetty

① Balanus balanoides barnacles on new jetty

fossil shells

coltsfoot

Thomas Telford's pier

Chthamalus barnacles

②

③ old boat

reed beds

oak keel

N

E

Brae Lusta

④

channel wrack

rock pools with beadlet anemones

⑤

concrete

Loch Bay

oystercatchers sat on rocks

⑥

nodular algal limestone

Sites of Interest

1. Jetty (NG263563)
New jetty intercepts longshore drift causing build-up of beach deposits on north-west side. After warm settled weather in mid-summer, red algae in surface water may flash when disturbed at night

2. Remains of old pier (NG263562)
Thomas Telford's pier built in 1798 using revolutionary new cement that could set under water

3. Ruined cottage (NG264562)
Limestone blocks in walls with bore-holes caused by piddocks. Old boat with *Caloplaca* lichen growing on deck

4. Three boulders (NG264560)
Large dolerite erratics on the mid-shore with zones of marine lichens and barnacles. Tiny pits in barnacle plates caused by lichens that have dissolved the surface.

5. Limestone lenticle (NG265558)
Pale-coloured limestone erratic with radula marks from a grazing limpet. Limestone surface favours growth of green seaweed

6. Oyster beds (NG266558)
Beds of extinct oysters eroding from cliff. Blocks of nodular algal limestone at top of shore

Thirty minutes had flown by. It was time to turn back after what had been the perfect pre-prandial walk.

Notes

The fossils found at Loch Bay belong to the Duntulm Formation (previously known as the Lower Ostrea Beds). They are characterised by thick beds of oysters interleaved with nodular algal limestone, which indicates marine-brackish conditions. The lower sections of the formation contain *Neomiodon* and *Unio* which are bivalves found in freshwater.

Fossils belonging to the Great Estuarine Group occur in the same sequence in several sites. These range from Trotternish in north Skye to Eigg over 90 kilometres away in the south. This suggests that the sediments were laid down in one continuous basin stretching across the Minch. The sequence of shells suggests a pattern of shallow freshwater lagoons occasionally breached by the invading sea.

The reference to a boat being sent from Harris to Loch Bay to collect limestone is taken from *A Tour through the Highlands of Scotland and the Hebride Isles in 1786* by John Knox, reprinted 1975 by James Thin; The Mercat Press, Edinburgh, pp 148-149.

References to Parker's Cement and the construction of Telford's pier can be found in *The British Fisheries Society 1786-1893* by Jean Dunlop; John Donald Publishers, Edinburgh, 1978. p.89.

7. Two Churches' Walk

Checklist

Distance	1.8 miles/2.9km
Approximate time	Allow one hour
Maps	1:25 000 OS Explorer 407
Terrain	Well-maintained paths and forest tracks
Special considerations	The approach to Site 4 is off the main forest path and is undertaken at your own risk. Dunvegan Castle Estate cannot accept responsibility for any injuries that may result in crossing the old plank bridge
Footwear	Boots
Parking	Roadside parking at the start enough for 3 or 4 cars (NG255477). Alternatively, ample parking available in the public car park in Dunvegan centre

When it's too windy to get out of the car, and too wet for the sheep to sit down, head for Dunvegan. There is a walk that is hidden amongst the trees that will save the day. It starts out on the old golf course, now no more except for the occasional imaginary bunker. It visits the ruins of St Mary's Church, then strides out briefly over an exposed moor before scurrying back into a grateful tunnel of trees, so dense and sheltered you feel you almost need a torch.

This is undoubtedly the most sheltered walk in north-west Skye. I remember leaving Glendale in a Force 10 south-westerly where you had to park facing the wind if you wanted to keep the car door. But Dunvegan offered a different world: half way round the Two Churches' Walk I could actually open the umbrella!

The start of the walk leading towards St Mary's Church

The traditional start to this walk is a quarter of a mile out from the centre of Dunvegan on the Portree road (if the weather is really severe, you can start at the opposite end and get straight into the woodland). The path leads to a series of information boards inside a walled enclosure and then passes the ruins of **St Mary's Church** which is the burial place of the Clan Macleod.

Continue following the path around the side of the churchyard. The grassy field to your left has the corrugated pattern known as **'runrig'** where once the ground was cultivated in strips, chiefly for potatoes. If the weather is clear, make your way across the field and climb to the top of the basalt outcrop on which is sited the Duirinish Millennium Stone (**site 1**).

Return to the footpath and continue through the gate. To the right you will find the deep purple flowers of **bell heather**, the first of the heathers to bloom. There are great views of the Cuillin over your right shoulder and the Isle of Rum behind, but they can be seen anytime. Today it's pouring down and it's all about looking at things in close-up.

Pass through the gate and look closely at the fence posts on your left (**site 2**). Notice how the lichens grow on the top but not lower down. What stops their progress is the rusting wire. Iron is toxic to most lichens and immediately below the rusting staples the wood is bare of growth.

Continue on, underneath the electric **power lines**, past the scented **bog myrtle** on the right, past an old overgrown wall which extends across to the slopes half a mile away to your right – to join an ancient enclosure surrounding a stand of **dead trees**, their trunks and branches bleached white like bare bones.

A gate leads into a plantation with scattered birch, rowan and hazel. Here in autumn you find turkey tail fungus growing on some of the tree stumps (**site 3**). The rowan and birch are covered in purple liverwort (*Frullania tamariski*). A line of hazels brings you to a bare rock 'lay-by'. There are blackberries everywhere and you wish it was September.

Look carefully to the right of the path for a fenced enclosure which houses some old water tanks. A rickety plank bridge crosses a stream

Looking towards Macleod's Tables from St Mary's Church

to reach the closed gate. Carefully approach the gate and look for an old decaying birch to the right of the plank bridge (**site 4**).

If it was down south, this tree would probably be inside the enclosure and guarded by CCTV cameras. It is a lichenologist's paradise. If you have never taken an interest in lichen before, this is the moment to shed all inhibitions. It is home to a group of lichen called 'The Lobarion'.

It sounds like something out of the *The Lord of the Rings*, something you wouldn't want to disturb. But the way to calm fear is through knowledge. If you can name the beasts, you have power over them. The names are good and well-worth learning if only to impress your companions afterwards in the bar. They are: *Lobaria pulmonaria* or 'lungwort', which looks apple-green on top and pale cream underneath and has the appearance of a freshly dissected lung; *Pseudocyphellaria crocata*, also known as the 'yellow speckled-belly lichen' because it resembles a bloated belly – grey brown to reddish, and, of course, green when wet with custard-coloured spots and ridges. And then there is *Sticta fuliginosaa* which resembles a

above left: Yellow speckled-belly lichen at site 4
right: 'Lobarion' lichens: *Degelia* (top); *Sticta* (centre); *Lobaria* (bottom)

desiccated prune, only it smells of rotting fish when squeezed between the fingers. And for the connoisseur there is *Degelia plumbea* which used to be called *Parmeliella plumbea* and looks like a flattened rosette carved out of a lump of lead, hence *plumbea.*

For all the daunting names, this covering of Latin on this decaying tree indicates unpolluted Atlantic air. It's what Skye has in abundance. You may not experience weather like this anywhere else, but that's why the lichens grow here!

Continue following the path as it passes a prickly section with wild raspberries and Canadian salmonberry (*Rubus spectabilis*). This plant was first introduced at the Castle and has since spread to many gardens in Skye.

'Tunnel' entrance at site 6

Look for a narrow **path junction** that branches off to the left (the track you have been following leads down to the road). The path gently climbs a basalt slope in a series of zig-zags.

Look for two unusually-large specimens of *Griselinia littoralis* to the left of the path. This plant comes from New Zealand, where it is known as **'shining broadleaf'**. It usually grows on the sea shore. Here it is thriving 200 metres above sea level.

Looking back, if it is clear, there is an unusual view of Dunvegan castle framed between a silver birch and a sycamore

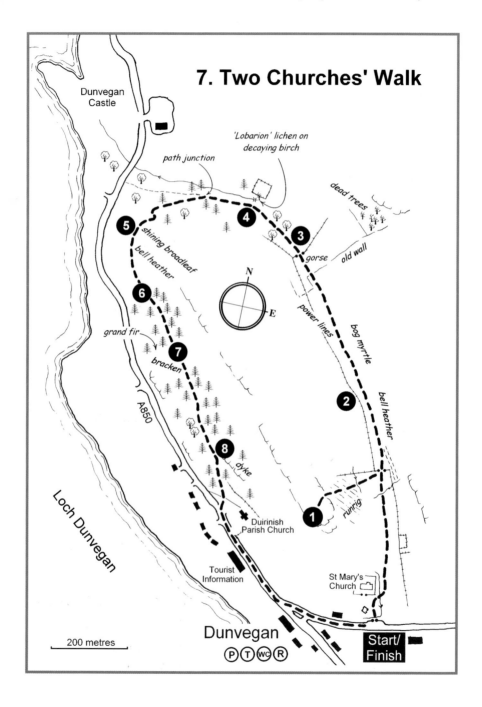

7. Two Churches' Walk

Dunvegan Castle

'Lobarion' lichen on decaying birch

path junction

dead trees

5

shining broadleaf

4

3

gorse   old wall

bell heather

6

N

E

power lines

bog myrtle

grand fir

7

bracken

2

bell heather

A850

8

dyke

1

runrig

Duirinish Parish Church

Loch Dunvegan

Tourist Information

St Mary's Church

Dunvegan

200 metres

Ⓟ Ⓣ ⓌⒸ Ⓡ

Start/ Finish

Sites of Interest

1. The Duirinish Stone (NG253479)
Stone collected from shore at Elgol erected to celebrate the Millennium. Fine viewpoint across Loch Dunvegan to Macleod's Tables

2. Fence posts (NG253483)
Toxic effect of iron and zinc affects the pattern of lichen growth fence wire and staples

3. Fungi and liverworts (NG252486)
Turkey tails and other fungi growing on birch, rowan together with copper coloured liverworts

4. 'The Lobarion' (NG250487)
Rare lichens growing on decaying birch indicate moist pollution-free air

5. Viewpoint (NG248487)
Unusual view of Dunvegan Castle

6. Tunnel of trees (NG248486)
Collection of southern hemisphere trees including Chilean lantern flower and New Zealand holly

7. Bracken-filled clearing (NG249484)
Grand fir (leaves smell of oranges) growing amongst Sitka spruce

8. Lime tree (NG251481)
A solitary lime tree with unusual blade-shaped branches near a volcanic dyke

(**site 5**). This open area allows good views across Loch Dunvegan. The green buoy floating in the main channel is a warning marker for mariners, indicating a sunken wreck.

The walk now enters a dense woodland (**site 6**). On the right, a huge Monteray cypress has blown over. On the left is an old larch with tangled branches covered in green beards of *Usnea* lichen. Then on the right another southern hemisphere species – the Chilean lantern flower, *Crinodendron hookeranum*, with large red flowers and leaves arranged in groups of three. This is followed on the left by a New Zealand holly, *Olerea macrodonta* reaching gigantic proportions and then an equally massive specimen of *Escallonia* alongside a yellow azalea.

Southern hemisphere now gives way to Sitka spruce, planted so dense that hardly any light filters down to the needle-clad floor. Alongside the path are what look like rotting tree stumps about 20 centimetres high. They are the decaying bases of the scaly male fern (*Dryopteris felix-mas*). Twenty years ago, they would have been crowned with a shuttlecock growth of lime-green leaves but now the light has gone, only the decaying bases remain.

Suddenly you reach a bracken-filled clearing (**site 7**), kept free of trees for the overhead power lines. Twenty metres below the path on the right, along the cleared edge, three trees stand out from the surrounding spruce. The foliage is darker and the branches fan out in horizontal layers. This is **grand fir** (*Abies grandis*). Bruise the needles between your fingers and they smell of oranges.

The path continues through the wood, past even closer lines of spruce. There is a native tree hidden amongst them – a single lime a few metres to the left of the path (**site 8**). Its side branches have become entangled together to produce a remarkable sculptured effect. This also marks the site of a dolerite **dyke** that has intruded through the basalt parallel with the path. The pressure of being confined within the basalt causes the crystal structure to become aligned sideways and the slow rate of cooling produces columnar jointing. The ends of the columns can be seen as hexagons and pentagons in the vertical face of the wall.

Some of the cracks between the columns are occupied by ferns. The brittle erect stems that look like fishes' backbones are from the hard fern (*Blechnum spicant*). The spores can be seen in rows along the underside of the 'backbone'. The softer leaves at the base of the plant are infertile and carry no spores. Look also for the broad buckler fern (*Dryopteris austriaca*) which has a dark narrow groove running along the back of each stem.

The path emerges from the dark wood outside the **Duirinish Parish Church**. Before leaving, count the number of church windows. All is not what it seems!

8. Coral Beaches

Checklist

Distance	2.5 miles/4km
Approximate time	Allow 2 hours
Maps	1:25 000 OS Explorer 407. 1:50 000 British Geological Survey, Sheet 80(W)
Terrain	Mostly on level tracks and over grassy foreshore
Equipment and Books	Sea shore and bird guide, binoculars, hand lens
Special considerations	If you wish to cross over onto Lampay, consult local tide tables beforehand
Footwear	Walking shoes are adequate in dry weather. Wellingtons should be taken if you wish to explore Lampay
Parking	Car park at Claigan (NG232537)

Visitors to north Skye don't usually come here for the beaches. It's not known for its buckets and spades and swimming in the sea. If you do find a sheltered bay, it's more likely to be chocked full of rocks and pebbles and the occasional stretch of black volcanic sand.

It will therefore come as a surprise to find a little patch of the Bahamas north of Dunvegan. Here is a beach that glistens pure white, shelving into a sea that is turquoise blue. The only thing missing are the palm trees.

The single-track road north of Dunvegan Castle leads you unerringly there, through dense woodland, a sharp chicane, cattle-grid, past a small cove just below the road on the left where once lay the wreck of an old wooden sailing boat, now mostly gone except for the occasional plank and a section of mast; past the seal islands, one with a bright

The approach to the Coral Beaches

green grass top, green because of the nesting arctic and common terns and a rogue black-back gull looking for unguarded eggs, past another island covered in common seals sunning themselves; and then on past reed beds with a freshwater loch on the right complete with tufted duck, goldeneye, pochard, mallard and in winter as many as 20 whooper swans. Today it's summer. The swans have all gone but the buzzards are out, circling above the backdrop of spruce.

The road ends at the car park. If you want to avoid the crowds, go early morning or mid week in winter. There is an information board telling you about the true nature of the beaches, explaining that they are in fact composed of bleached seaweed, locally known as maerl, and scientifically known as *Lithothamnion*.

The path is really an old track, built to transport the coral when it was used for agricultural lime. Chemical analysis has shown that it contains 84 per cent calcium carbonate and 10 percent magnesium carbonate. Boring! This isn't a day for chemistry. This is a day to enjoy the sun, sea and wildlife.

The track passes a thicket of gorse and then an area of bog myrtle on the right. There is a group of old cairns (**site 1**) hidden from view on the left before reaching an iron gate. The level track leads to a wide grassy area with silverweed and ox-eye daisy. Cross the stream close to the shoreline, past the ruined **walls** where boats were once hauled ashore. Note that the path is indistinct along this section.

Follow the shoreline, out of sight of the main path. This is what the otters do. After swimming in the sea, they like to wash themselves in fresh water to remove the salt from their fur. Look carefully around the margins of several small pools (**site 2**) sunk into the grassy shelf above the shore. Here you will find bright green mounds of grass topped with grey and black spraints. (During dry weather, these pools will dry out and only damp hollows will remain.)

Follow the coast until you reach a well-trodden path taking you along the side of a low cliff and then down a **rocky descent** to the bowling-alley-smooth grass track that follows the shore, eventually to join a rutted farm track.

Raised beach with layers of sand and shells (site 4)

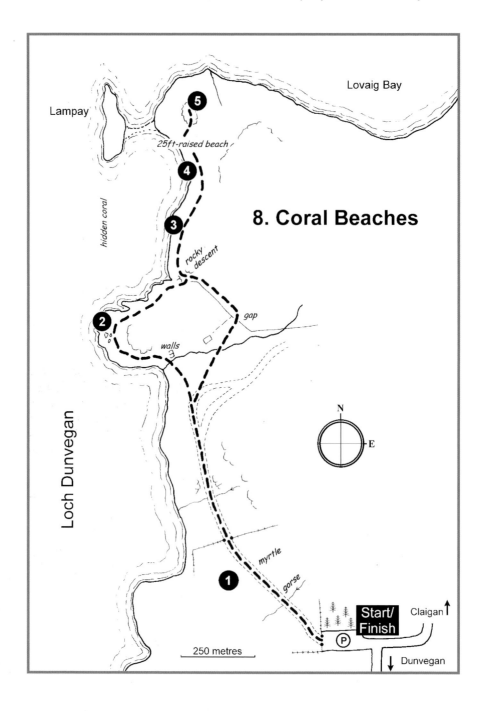

8. **Coral Beaches**

Lovaig Bay

Lampay

25ft-raised beach

hidden coral

rocky descent

gap

walls

Loch Dunvegan

N
E

myrtle

gorse

Start/
Finish

Claigan

Dunvegan

250 metres

Sites of Interest

1. **Old cairns (NG229538)**
   Group of overgrown clearance cairns

2. **Fresh-water pools (NG223545)**
   Remote site frequented by otters

3. **Dolerite dyke (NG224547)**
   Prominent 'walls' of rock with bird pellets and otter spraints

4. **Former beach deposits (NG223550)**
   Horizon of shells provides evidence of 25ft-raised beach

5. **Viewpoint (NG223552)**
   Basalt crag with views west of hidden coral and north to the islands of Isay, Mingay and Clett

This is easy, level ground. Notice the volcanic dykes where the harder dolerite intruded into the basalt (**site 3**). They look like sections of eroded stone walls. The top of the dykes are worth examining, just where a bird would perch. Here the grass is darker with traces of shells that have decayed out from regurgitated pellets left by herring gulls. There may also be signs of otters on the highest points.

The coral bay looks more intriguing the closer you get. If it's windy from the west, you will be caught in a storm of drifting sand as it blows across the grass foreshore. This flat platform is marked on the geology map as a 25-foot raised beach. It was once lapped by the high tide and is full of shells and sand from days when it used to be the original coral beach. You can see the horizontal layers of beach trapped in the soil where it has become exposed along its edge (**site 4**). After the Ice Age, after the pressure of ice had gone, the land rebounded back to its present height above the tide line.

The scurrying white birds picking their way along the water's edge in spring are ringed plover. The small brown birds walking amongst the seaweed strands at the top of the shore – the dull brown ones that you pass by without a second glance – are rock pipits: slightly darker plumage and darker legs than meadow pipits.

The brown seaweed amongst the coral is the knotted wrack, *Ascopyllum nodosum* – an indicator of sheltered water. The more sheltered the water, the more floatation bladders or 'knots'. On exposed shores, the fronds are kept separated by wave action, and floatation bladders are moribund.

There are masses of coral just offshore, only you don't see it. A diver friend of mine told me that a typical Skye coastline would have a steep basalt cliff disappearing into the sea, below which a sloping boulder-field would lead into a bright pink band of coral about 10 to 20 metres below mean low water.

Why then does it appear above high tide in so few places in Skye? (The other main site is near Ord in Sleat.) There are a number of factors shared by these sites. Both are mostly west-facing with strong tidal currents. They are often connected to an offshore island by a spit of land that becomes exposed at low tide. This results in the disruption of the tidal flow or longshore drift.

At Dunvegan, the beach material builds up on the north side of the spit whilst broken pieces of dead coral accumulate in the regions of slack, shallow water on the south side. A beach is then able to develop

Looking across to Lampay island at low tide

as the tide and the prevailing winds carry the fragments inshore. At low tide you can walk across the narrow spit of land to the island of **Lampay** but keep a close watch on the next tide as it can soon cut off your retreat.

To get an overall view of the geography, take the path to the top of the rock 'table' that overlooks the bay (**site 5**). From here you will also see the extent of the **hidden coral** beds giving the sea a pale green colour. This vantage point also gives you a fine view north to the islands of Isay, Mingay and Clett.

You will need your binoculars here. Isay is basalt. It is the largest of the three, with a flat area of basalt-covered grass with sheep. It was offered to Dr Johnson by the Clan Chief of MacLeod if he agreed to stay there "three months in the year; nay one month". The good doctor thought long and hard about it but declined. It is now a favourite residence for barnacle geese.

Mingay is dolerite: harder rock than basalt, fracturing into nice ledges, attracting cormorants which sit on its skyline and shags that seem more comfortable on the

Live coral (*Lithothamnion*) is coloured red but is bleached white when it dies

ledges below. The volcanic rock rests on a bed of Jurassic shale and limestone which was once excavated and processed in the limekiln on its east shore. There used to be black rabbits living near the kiln, but the keen-eyed buzzard that nests on the cliff above was probably their nemesis. In May the island develops a sheen of blue from its covering of bluebells.

Clett is also made of dolerite and provides fine ledges for nesting shag, cormorant, common guillemot and razorbill. The more gentle southwest-facing shore is a favourite resting place for common seals.

Just out from the shore, there is always the chance of spotting gannets, eider ducks, arctic and common terns and black guillemot.

If the wildlife doesn't appear, try spotting Dun Hallin on the Waternish peninsula. It is one of the best preserved duns in Skye.

Notes

The offer of Isay to Dr Johnson is recalled in *The Journal of a Tour to the Hebrides with Samuel Johnson LLD* by James Boswell, Everyman's Library, Dent, 1909. p.237.

There are three different types of coral or maerl: *Phymatolithon calcareum* is found only in marine conditions whilst *Lithothamnion coralloides* and *L. glaciale* will grow in estuaries where there is an input of fresh water.

There is a rich variety of molluscs growing in the silty deposits alongside the maerl. This is reflected in the large number of shells found washed up on the coral beach. Examples include otter shell, rayed artemis, venus shell, and numerous cockles. Many are overgrown with white calcareous tubes which are home to various bristle worms. Those with a triangular cross-section are made by *Pomatoceros triqueter*, whilst circular cross-sections are from *Serpula vermicularis*. The seaweeds are often found encrusted with tiny spiral shells secreted by the *Spirorbis* worm.

9. Neist Point

Checklist

Distance	1.6 miles/2.5km
Approximate time	1 hour
Maps	1:25 000 OS Explorer 407. 1:50 000 British Geological Survey, Sheet 80(W)
Terrain	Steep footpath and steps lead to flat grassy sections. Cliff edges are sheer and care needed in high wind
Special considerations	Please park carefully so as not to restrict access to lighthouse garages
Footwear	Boots or walking shoes
Parking	Marked area at road end (NG133477)

Out here, you don't listen to the weather forecast. It can be sunny and calm in Portree. It can be pleasantly warm with a gentle breeze in Dunvegan. People in Glendale can be walking about normally in shirt sleeves and chatting casually outside the Post Office. And all the while, there is a Force 8 blowing at Neist with stratus down to 100 metres and you don't go outside for fear of being hit by someone's roof.

This is the most westerly point in Skye. It catches all that the Atlantic can throw at us and more. Stand at the tip of Neist Point and you could imagine being in a boat with salt spray and spume being flung across your bows. Out here, you listen to the shipping forecast.

The walk starts from the road end. Take the lighthouse steps down. The handrail is there for a purpose. The rock you are passing is dolerite, a volcanic sill that has weathered into numerous boulders. Where the steps cut through is south-facing and dotted with bell heather, kidney vetch (with flowers like miniature bunches of bananas), wild thyme, and one prominent willow being eaten by the larva of a puss moth. At the end of the first line of steps, look

The Stallion Rock at Neist is home to fulmar, kittiwake and herring gulls

immediately down to your right (**site 1**). The rock is covered in green algae and has a scattering of fish bones and crab claws from weathered otter spraints.

Amongst the boulders to your left you will hear a wren and a male **stonechat** flitting from top to top. A wheatear starts its frantic alarm call: *wheat-chack-chack*. It means that a stoat is on the prowl looking for eggs or young.

At the bottom of the steep path you pass through a gap in a magnificently-constructed dolerite wall. Aim off diagonally right, passing three large boulders, each used by wheatears and rock pipits as lookout perches. (The lichens never lie!) The wall top has the same clues (see Notes).

Walk to the edge of the cliff (**site 2**) and you will see shag to your right, flying in low before finally rising onto their nesting ledges. Look left at the impressive cliff known as **The Stallion** with its wheeling **fulmar**, hanging in the updrafts, hanging just out from the edge before turning off to complete their carousel ride. They nest on the broad grassy ledges, lay a single egg, live for 14 years – which is exceptional for a bird of that size – and leave no guano on or below the nest.

Now, if you don't suffer from vertigo, go a little further-out and look back at the cliff below the wall. It is covered in the white flowers of scurvy grass. It grows well here because it is kept moist and well-nourished. Water drains down to the horizontal strata and is then directed to the cliff surface. The strata is Jurassic shale and limestone.

Now look in the opposite direction towards The Stallion. The same pale yellow-brown strata can be picked out half way up, where it runs out from the grass edge. It then curves upwards and disappears. Imagine a 'cheese sandwich' made from two slices of dolerite with shale in the middle. That's what you have behind you. What you see

Fulmar: the spitfire of the sea

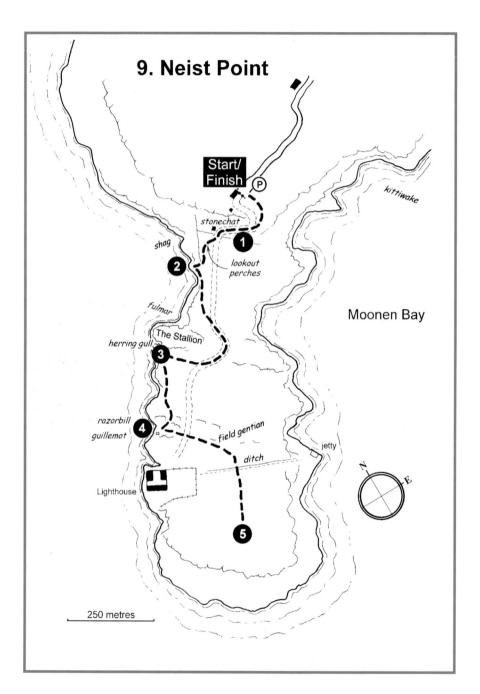

9. Neist Point

Start/Finish

kittiwake

stonechat

1

shag

2

lookout perches

fulmar

Moonen Bay

The Stallion

herring gull

3

razorbill

guillemot

4

field gentian

jetty

ditch

Lighthouse

5

250 metres

Sites of Interest

1. End of steps (NG132477)
Otter spraints on algae-covered rock

2. Cliff edge (NG130477)
Jurassic shale with intrusion of dolerite sill provides habitats for plant and bird life

3. Cliff face (NG128474)
Nesting herring gull and black backed gull

4. Cliff edge (NG127472)
Nesting ledges of razorbill, guillemot and kittiwake

5. Exposed grassland (NG127469)
Wind-blasted grassland with patches of bog pimpernel

---

in front is where someone has peeled away the top slice and then pushed their thumb through the bottom slice to make the bulge. The middle slice of cheese is then bent upwards before being broken through by the thumb (the molten lava). If you look at the base of the layer of cheese – where it has been bent – you will see that it has been baked white by the intense heat.

Continue along the cliff edge. Look left, half a mile across Moonen Bay. An area of the lower sill of dolerite (bottom slice of bread) has a number of white seabirds wheeling in front of it. You don't need a bird book. This cliff, with its narrow ledges covered in guano, says "**kittiwake**": totally different from the broad clean-kept ledges on The Stallion. Check them with binoculars. The bird is facing inwards towards the cliff (fulmar face outwards). You can hear them call in the wind: "kittiwake-kittiwake-kittiwake". They fly low with a delicate pronounced down beat. And then just to confirm it – pure black wing tips.

Briefly rejoin the path to climb over the side of The Stallion. Where the grass has a walkable gradient, contour across to the right to see what is on the south-facing side of this cliff (**site 3**). It's the first week in June. You can hear the high pitch calls of the chicks. A sloping rock face with ledges surrounded by thrift, scurvy grass and ox-eye daisies.

Adult **herring gulls** sit and stand everywhere. Look closely. A grey speckled chick pecks its parent's beak. Then another, and another appear making three in a nest.

The large black-winged gull nesting on the top of the crest of the rock face is a great black-back gull, looking for the eggs or unguarded chicks below. It too has to eat and feed its young.

Go further to the edge, if you are fearless of heights. Fulmar nest below the herring gulls. Kittiwakes disappear to nest just out of sight around the corner. A black guillemot, like a huge bumblebee with beetroot-red legs and a white oval on its wing, flies in only to disappear in a crack. Below, on the sea, a line of common guillemot and razorbill snake out across the surface. Which is which? The razorbill is soot-black with hunched shoulders. The guillemot is chocolate browny-black with a more stress-free neck, sometimes wearing white spectacles.

A group of shag fly low, within a metre of the sea surface, taking the long route round into **Moonen Bay**. How do you know they are shag and not cormorant? Because they are flying low. A cormorant would take the short cut and fly over land. Shags are more oceanic rather than estuarine.

Gannets dive. They have flown in from St Kilda – their nearest breeding colony. Sometimes they fly directly overhead, but that's rare. A dolphin appears, out where the tidal race forms a white line of up-welling food. And then two fins lazily flop from side to side, seemingly disconnected until you realise they belong to the same fish – a basking shark.

Follow the cliff to a white concrete tank on a vertiginous edge (**site 4**). Peer over to see a nesting shag, with lines of **razorbill**, **guillemot**, fulmar and kittiwake, all happily coexisting. Cross over the path and cut across a bare gravel slope where, in September, you will find field gentian, but only after nearly giving up.

Make your way across the wet peaty ground, but don't aim for the corner post of the lighthouse fence, where everybody else has walked and so-eroded the ground that it is almost as bare as sections of the Pennine Way.

Cross a deep ditch (care!) and enter the grassy area in the centre of the peninsula (**site 5**). The foghorn appears on your right but, thankfully, is no longer working. Where the ground looks the most

Close view of The Stallion with its curved layers of sandstone and shale

impoverished, wind-blasted and salt-laden – where no vascular plant in its right mind would grow – this is the place to get down on your hands and knees and look for cotton-thin threads of stem with pairs of round, tiny leaves and, in July through to September, an incredibly-beautiful candy-pink-striped, adjective-soaked flower known as bog pimpernel. It is rare and almost always overlooked. Other lost souls may be looking out to sea for a glimpse of a shearwater or a minke. But when the mist comes down, the bog pimpernel will always be there.

Notes

The tops of rocks and walls, that are regularly used by birds as lookout perches, often have a covering of the mustard yellow lichen *Candeleriella* spp., which belong to the 'Nutrient-Enriched' community of lichens.

10. Macleod's Maidens

Checklist

Distance	4.5 miles/7.3km
Approximate time	Allow 6 to 7 hours
Maps	1:25 000 OS Explorer 407
Terrain	Level, forest track then undulating narrow path across moor and grassland, mostly dry
Footwear	Boots
Parking	Car park at Orbost Farm (NG256432)

To the south of the Duirinish peninsula lies one of the finest stretches of coast in the country. The turning point is The Maidens – a group of sea stacks hidden from view until you are almost upon them.

After what seems like an interminable trek across a heather moor, you suddenly realise where you are, perched on top of a basalt cliff with sea eagles and fulmar for company.

This was the first time Janet had made the trip. I had done it numerous times, once or twice even returning by a circular route through Glen Ollisdal. "Why don't we make it a circular route?" she asked. But the voice of experience prevailed: "I think it will be enough to go there and back."

It was the start of the spring sunshine. It was so hot, we parked the car in the shade next to the wall at Orbost. The track leads alongside the wall with its sycamore trees drawn out sideways by the prevailing south westerlies (**site 1**). There are amazing views across Loch Bracadale all the way as you curve round towards Bharcasaig with its bay of black basalt sand. Pieces of pottery have been found in some of the rocky inlets: white teapots and tureens and plates with blue and red crosses and circles around their rims – washed ashore from the

Aerial photograph of the Maidens and the south Durinish peninsula showing the separate horizontal lava flows

sailing barge *Yemassee* that ran aground in 1859. The wreck is still hidden out there in the loch.

The track swings round above the bay and enters the remaining forestry plantation. This has been extensively felled and soon the views open out over Bracadale. The track leads through a gap in a well-constructed stone **wall (site 2)**. This wall is interesting. The stones next to the gap look normal but the rest looks as though it is made of a different rock – a dingy brown colour instead of the usual light grey. The light grey is a crustose lichen that requires uninterrupted sunlight in order to grow. The dingy brown is bare rock which up until recently has been kept in almost perpetual twilight. This hillside was once covered with dense rows of Sitka spruce. The wall reflects its past history.

After crossing a small stream, the forestry road ends just short of **Forse Burn**. In the past I have always taken an interest in this burn and ventured a short distance along it to see if there were any fossil leaves trapped between basalt lavas. This is where basalts from two different centres overlap. The lavas from these centres originated from vastly different periods in the geological record, allowing soils and vegetation to develop. The geology map indicates the site with a tantalising letter 'Zb' to indicate 'palagonite tuff'. Each time I have been here, I have searched for fossil leaves and wood and each time I have drawn a blank, finding only the bright red iron oxides that characterise the top of a basalt lava flow.

Once over the burn, the path continues through a gate and climbs to the right indicated by a waymark arrow. It continues climbing for several hundred metres along the side of a valley, with the sound of the burn a constant companion on the right. And then, where the path levels out, the noise of running water suddenly stops and there is silence. The path now drops down towards the deserted village above **Brandersaig Bay** into a fenced area that has recently been planted with native birch and named **'Rebel Wood'**. This is where the first stonechats appear.

Looking south-east over Macleod's Maidens towards the Cuillin (Photograph: © Hugh MacLeod 2010)

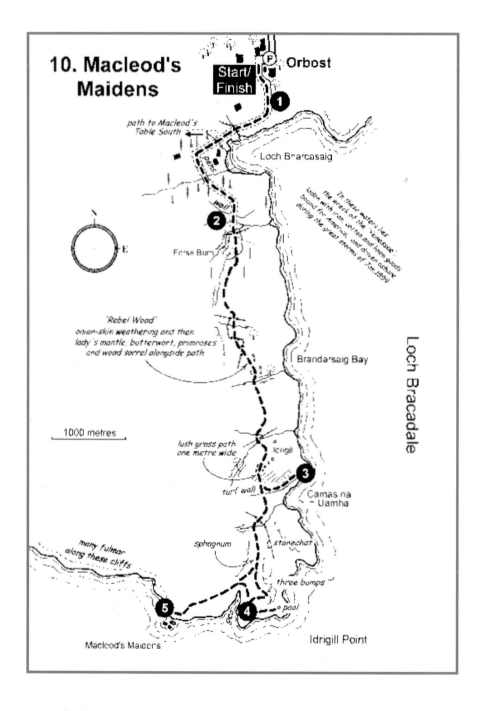

10. Macleod's Maidens

Orbost

Start/Finish

path to Macleod's Table South

Loch Brarcasaig

In these waters lies the wreck of the Teresuse Luton with iron, salt pan and linen goods bound for America, and driven ashore during the great storms of 1 Jan 1898

N

E

Forse Burn

'Rebel Wood' onion-skin weathering and then lady's mantle, butterwort, primroses and wood sorrel alongside path

Brandarsaig Bay

Loch Bracadale

1000 metres

lush grass path one metre wide

Icrigill

Camas na Uamha

turf wall

many fulmar along these cliffs

sphagnum

stonechat

three bumps

pool

Macleod's Maidens

Idrigill Point

Sites of Interest

1. **Sycamore trees (NG258428)**
   Line of 'flag trees' drawn out in one direction indicating
   prevailing south-westerlies

2. **Stone wall (NG249409)**
   Covering of white and grey lichens indicate where surface has
   been exposed to sunlight. Dingy brown surface indicates areas
   kept in shadow by dense spruce plantation recently cleared

3. **Bay of the Caves (NG254376)**
   View of coast from area of deeply-incised runrig

4. **Geo viewpoint (NG247362)**
   Unusual sideways view of Maidens across deep coastal indent.
   Patches of mountain everlasting and thrift

5. **Maiden's viewpoint (NG244363)**
   Lofty view looking down to the Maidens

We followed a narrow path crossing a section of **onion-skin weathering**, before reaching the first ruined house on the left, with scaly male fern growing from the base of its walls. A well-placed seat encouraged us to stop for a coffee break, then it was on across a delightful stream with a wooded gorge with hazel and rowans and the sound of willow warblers and robins. The path climbed again, passing more grassed-over ruins and some prominent runrig on the left. The lush, green path happens to be a metre wide. Why should level paths in open countryside be such a precise width? Could it be that whenever possible, people prefer to walk in pairs, side-by-side?

After crossing the switchback of runrig, we came to a prominent **turf wall** that cut across the path. At this point we turned left away from the path and, after about 100 metres, we found ourselves at the edge of the cliff, with deeply incised runrig behind us and an amazing view across **Camas na h-Uamha** – the Bay of the Caves (**site 3**).

We returned to the main path, which led across the moor through a gate in a fence, passing a sheep pen with a **stonechat** calling from a

nearby post, then onwards, following a sunken section held between crags, over **sphagnum**, passing three bumps on the skyline to our left. The third bump on a rocky knoll had crowberry and bird pellets with localised patches of mouse-ear. We dropped down to the huge **geo** that opened out below (**site 4**). Mountain everlasting in one patch – short turf and thrift everywhere else. This is windswept salt-laden ground. A privilege to be here on a sunny windless day with the first views of the Maidens about to hit us.

This is where you need plenty of space on the digital camera and make sure the battery is well charged. Midday into the sun – set camera 2 stops underexposed. Perfect silhouettes. Black angular bands of rock floating in a grey, still sea. You hardly notice South Uist beyond.

A single rock with a **pool** of water was the spot for lunch. Not a soul in sight. Not even a herring gull waiting to pick up scraps.

Now it was time to cross over to the end of the cliff above the **Maidens** (**site 5**). The view has been photographed and published many times but it still takes you by surprise. This is where the fulmars fly, nesting on ledges, looking out. This is where the eagles fly, looking for fulmar. When you see two birds approaching one another and suddenly two birds become one and the one continues its flight without changing its speed, without losing height – the phrase 'effortless superiority' comes to mind.

You could stay here all day, watching the birds, but sooner or later you have to get back. It's a long haul. Whatever the distance shown on the map – double it. Whatever time you think it will be before reaching the car – double it. It's a hard slog across the moor but it marks the end of a day you won't forget.

Looking down on Macleod's Maidens (site 5)

11. Oronsay

Checklist

Distance	2.9 miles/4.7km
Approximate time	Allow 2 to 3 hours
Maps	1:25 000 OS Explorer 410
Terrain	Boggy on the mainland but then dry grassy paths with easy gradients on Oronsay
Special considerations	Consult local tide tables before setting out
Footwear	Boots
Parking	Follow narrow road east from Ullinish Lodge Hotel and after 300 metres turn right at the junction. There is a parking lay-by, 500 metres further on the left at the end of the road (NG322374)

If you are looking for a sunset with sea and islands and a lighthouse, Loch Bracadale takes some beating. At the centre of this calendar image is the tidal island of Oronsay.

This 'island' has one of the sharpest cliffs, some of the finest grass, and a line of sea stacks with colonies of breeding shag, fulmar and herring gull that are hardly ever visited. In the space of a mile you can walk from croft land, looking inland, across a narrow causeway of pebbles to be surrounded by the sea. Normally such transitions are only possible by boat.

If you want to get away from it all and become more familiar with barnacles and the territorial signs of an otter, this is the place to be. Leave the car behind for a few hours and take the crossing to Oronsay.

Many years ago we had walked onto Oronsay when the kids were young and we were worried about going too close to the cliff edge.

Back then, we had a memorable day pottering about near the causeway and amongst the rock pools on its south-eastern side. Now we returned with friends, *sans enfants*, and were able to explore the island's scary heights along its northern and western edge.

We took the road east of the Ullinish Lodge Hotel and turned right along the narrow side road and parked at the end. It was the new moon on a cold late April afternoon. It had to be the afternoon because we had checked the tide tables. April was a good month and the new moon ensured we caught the maximum spring tide.

Our seafaring friend knows about these things. He explained we had a good three hours of safety before being cut off – something about the Rule of Twelfths. The tide comes in following a sigmoid time scale. First hour it rises one twelfth of its range, second hour two twelfths, followed by three twelfths and three twelfths again, and then you start running.

The muddy path led across flat grassland following an old wall past some old **cairns** and stone ruins. After passing a gate through a fence, the path led around the rim of a steep-sided bay with gorse and rowan

Photographing the sunset over Oronsay from a favourite viewpoint off the A863 Broadford-Struan road north of Gesto. The sea stacks at the toe of Oronsay can be seen to the right of the lighthouse on Ardtreck Point

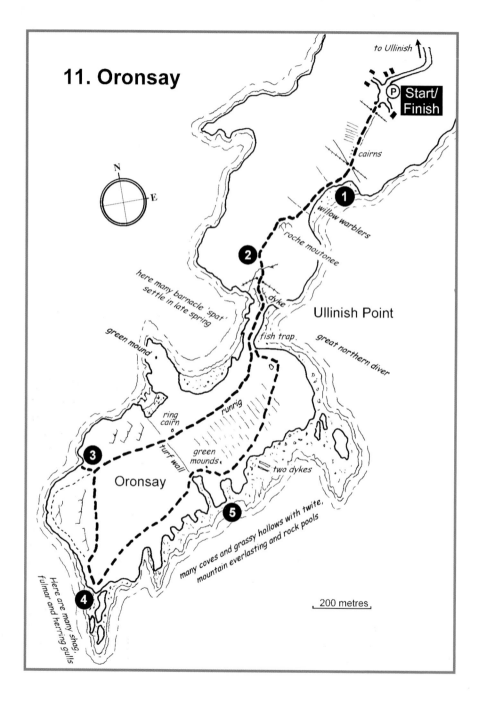

11. Oronsay

to Ullinish

P Start/Finish

cairns

N

E

① willow warblers

roche moutonee

②

here many barnacle 'spat' settle in late spring

dyke

Ullinish Point

green mound

fish trap

great northern diver

ring cairn

runrig

③

green mounds

turf wall

Oronsay

two dykes

⑤

many coves and grassy hollows with twite, mountain everlasting and rock pools

④

Here are many shag, fulmar and herring gulls

200 metres

Sites of Interest

1. **Tree-fringed bay (NG321370)**
   Gorse, rowan and willow warblers

2. **Peat bog (NG319365)**
   Old peat cuts with sphagnum and hair's tail cotton grass

3. **Cliff edge (NG312360)**
   View west across Loch Bracadalet to Wiay and Macleod's Maidens

4. **Viewpoint (NG310356)**
   The 'toe' of the island with views down to stacks with nesting shag, fulmar and herring gull

5. **Coves and arches (NG315360)**
   Sheltered coastline with twite, otter spraints, and rock pools

and the sound of **willow warblers (site 1)**. The path crossed two faint turf walls and then as it started to climb, Janet shouts back that she thinks we are crossing a *roche moutonnée*. Which was the cue for me retelling the story of how geologists consistently call these features 'stone sheep' based on an error in translation. A *moutonnée* is an eighteenth-century French wig made of fleece, like the ones Handel used to wear. All the curls run in one direction. Moving ice smoothes and plucks the rock to form what look like lop-sided 'curls'. It's nothing to do with sheep, but then, what can you do?

We continued climbing past some scrubby willow to get our first view of Oronsay with the leaning headland of Rubha nan Clach forming a dramatic backdrop. Next we crossed a very boggy section with old peat cuts, surrounded by sphagnum and deer sedge and the occasional hare's tail cotton grass (**site 2**).

After a gate, the path cut steeply down a rock gully formed along the margin of a dolerite **dyke**. The right-hand wall was covered in the grey-green tufts of sea ivory. Now we were on the shingle and pebble beach with an outcrop of red basalt. This type of rock is usually

crumbly, often developing on the exposed top of a basalt lava flow where it becomes filled with crystal-lined gas bubbles, but here, the contact with the dolerite had baked it hard and transformed its entire crystal structure.

The tide was out and the rocky outcrops on the right were covered in barnacles. But being aware of time and tide, we rushed on to the island, passing the white beaches on either side; past an ancient **fish trap** – exposed on the left as an enclosing low stone wall; up onto pebbles with silverweed growing in between; climbing onto a platform of grass with a foundation that looked like a raised beach, complete with flat and edible periwinkles, buried in the soil. Was this why the grass looked so fertile?

Stones the size of cricket balls littered the grass surface, way back from the sea. We speculated that they had been flung here by the gales of January 2005, when parts of Dunvegan and Waternish were devastated and we had power cuts for five days. Five days!

We passed more **runrig**; and then, forty metres before reaching a **turf wall**, a sunken **ring cairn** appeared to the right of the path. A faint track climbed towards the cliffs along the north-west edge with dramatic views of Wiay and Macleod's Maidens (**site 3**).

We followed a left-hand branch that kept low and aimed for the south-west tip of the island. Suddenly the western cliff edge was reached, with its fulmar and herring gulls, 200 feet above sea level. We made our way to the island's toe where a line of stacks suddenly appeared (**site 4**): masses of seabirds and yellow lichens; shags resting on the furthest point; mating herring gulls on the rock platform below; and a solitary great black-backed gull standing watch on a teetering spire. You need a head for heights to stand here with binoculars.

After a flask of coffee surrounded by bucks-horn plantain and thrift, we made our return journey, exploring the geos and indents along the south-east shore (**site 5**). This was a delightful section with grassy tables and U-shaped coves and rock arches with scurvy grass and primrose in flower; and dark mounds of grass to keep the otter-spotters on their mettle; and unexpected patches of 'mountain everlasting' for the botanist to touch; and twite for the bird watcher to try and distinguish the male from the female by looking for its pink rump; and rock pools with beadlet anemones to bring back memories of what rock pools used to be ...

Aerial photograph of Oronsay and Loch Bracadale

Hollows and coves along the south side of Oronsay (site 5)

But the Rule of Twelfths was hanging over us. We had to get back or stay the night. A great northern diver held up progress but we eventually made our crossing back onto the 'mainland'.

There was one last look at the barnacles with a hand-lens before the tide covered them, when – surprise! Barnacle spat! The new moon had been the trigger for one of the great seasonal maritime events. When the moon is right, barnacle larvae suddenly settle in their millions and colonise exposed surfaces on the shore. Within hours, the free-swimming sesame-seed-shaped cyprid larvae had glued themselves head-down to the rock and became transformed into young barnacles. When you've seen that, there's not much else to say.

12. Preshal Beg

Checklist

Distance	6 miles/9.7km
Approximate time	6 hours
Maps	1:25 000 OS Explorer 411
Terrain	After leaving the Talisker Bay track, the path is ill-defined and great care should be taken on the steep ascent and when approaching the cliff-top sections. There is no distinct footpath on the return route from Preshal Beg. The route to the broch is wet and featureless and care is needed to navigate the correct course from the broch to Sleadale Burn
Equipment	OS map and compass
Special considerations	**This walk is not recommended in mist or with children**
Footwear	Boots
Parking	Parking pace in the turning area at NG326306. Please park carefully so as to avoid blocking entrance drives

You may read about somewhere in a guide book and be disappointed when you see it for yourself. Preshal Beg is different.

The first record of this geological feature is found in Thomas Pennant's 1772 Tour in Scotland. He called it 'Briis-mhawl', which is how he would have heard the name 'Preshal' in Gaelic. The reason for his visit was to see "the most northern Basaltes ... the last of four in the British dominions, all running from South to North, nearly in a meridian: the Giant's Causeway appears first; Staffa succeeds; the rock Humbla about twenty leagues further, and finally the column of Briis-

mhawl; the depth of the ocean in all probability conceal the lost links of this chain."

    Boswell and Johnson, also paid a visit to Talisker on their tour in 1773. Boswell recalls – "After dinner [Coll] and I walked to the top of Prieshwell, a very high rocky hill, from whence there is a view of Barra, - the Long Island, - Bernera, - the Loch of Dunvegan, part of Rum – part of Rasay, and a vast deal of the isle of Sky." Boswell was referring to Preshal More, which is much closer to the laird's house, and would certainly have been a more reasonable goal to attempt "after dinner".

On a bright April morning, we set out from the parking area at Talisker. The first things you notice are the magnificent horse chestnut and sycamore trees along the boundary wall facing you (**site 1**). Their bark is more alkaline than oak or birch and older trees

The shimmering sea and surf of Talisker Bay seen from the climb to site 3

usually have a characteristic covering of lichens mosses and ferns. Here we found some magnificent growths of lungwort, *Lobaria pulmonaria*, crinkly-green leaves, white underneath, with chestnut brown discs bubbling up all over its surface – a nationally-scarce lichen that is fairly common in western Scotland.

We followed the road with the wall on our right. The wall-top was covered in polypody fern. The magnificent rock towers of Preshal More loomed up on the skyline to our left. The way continued past Talisker House and garden with its fine specimen of Chile pine.

The road now became a track leading to Talisker Bay. You are already walking on what used to be the bay, or what geologists call a 'raised beach' that sprung back after the Ice Age-ice had melted. You can see the pebbles and beach debris along the left hand edge of the track (**site 2**).

At the end of the track, on the left and just before a gate, there is the **well** attributed to Cuchulin (**site 3**) – the legendary warrior who came over from Ireland. Some think he gave his name to the Cuillin but others, including Sheriff Nicolson, point out that hardly any of the Skye mountains are named after people, but are more likely to be derived from the names of plants and animals. On this basis, the spiky outline of the Cuillin would be derived from the Gaelic name for holly – *a' Chuilionn.*

The track to the bay goes through the gate and sweeps to the right, but we veered left where a faint path started-out along the line of the fence. Take care on this next section. This is the hardest part of the walk and needs a steady head for heights and confidence in your boots. A faint path leaves the fence and climbs steeply towards a gully where it heads in the direction of a small waterfall before looping back on itself. This is the way the otter takes. At each bend in the path, it had marked its way with **spraints**. You may feel like doing the same if you linger here too long. Someone has left their shoe here, which is being colonized nicely by moss.

We crossed the stream at the top of the gully and continued out towards the cliff edge, crossing a split in the ground full of **roseroot**. We carefully made our way to the edge where a line of sea stacks suddenly appeared: fantastic and totally unexpected. The tallest stack had a great black-back gull perched on top with yellow lichen below (**site 3**).

We moved along the cliff edge to a favourite perching site for sea birds. On a mound of dark green grass I found a **bird pellet**: a cluster

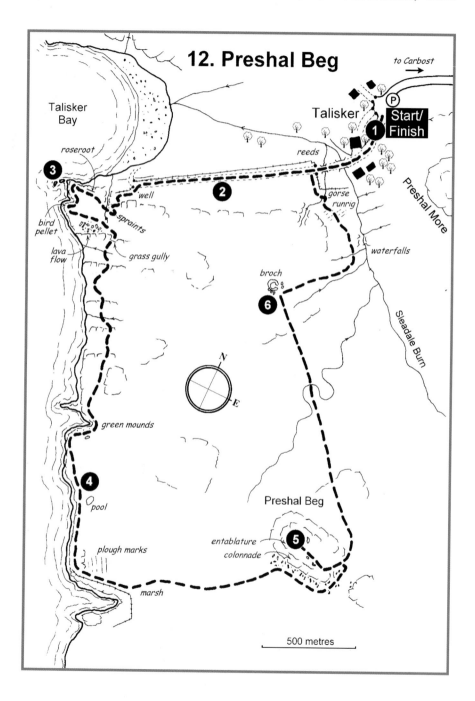

Sites of Interest

1. **Chestnut trees behind old wall (NG325305)**
   Spectacular growths of lungwort and polypody on tree bark
   and wall-top

2. **Raised beach (NG321300)**
   Rounded pebbles and beach deposits from former shore line

3. **Sea stacks (NG311299)**
   Cliff-top viewpoint with seabird nests and perching sites

4. **Biod Ruadh (NG319281)**
   Highest section of sea cliff with extensive views across north
   Skye and the Minch

5. **Preshal Beg (NG329279)**
   Prismatic 'colonnade' of basalt covered by 'entablature'

6. **Broch (NG323291)**
   Outer walls with impressive entrance and lintel leading to
   collapsed gallery and cell

of rough periwinkles, a bone of unknown origin, and wonder of
wonders – an intact shell from a blue-rayed limpet, its blue rays still
glinting in the sun.

This was the perfect place for a break: time to ponder the band of
rocks to the south – what looked like a Greek temple. Its ruined façade
could easily have been constructed from columns of white marble but
was in fact the mid-section of a **lava flow** with a surface hard enough
to support a continuous layer of white crabs eye lichen. We walked
below the line of the lava flow inland where a **grass gully** allowed an
easy ascent.

The route now followed the cliff at a sensible distance from the
edge. This is not the place to wander if you have vertigo. Eventually
we reached a dramatic cleft or 'geo'. Around its edge were four **green**

Approaching the 'impregnable fortress' of Preshal Beg

mounds used as bird perches. Half-way down the cliff there was a band of prismatic jointing – another taster of what was to come.

We continued climbing to what is the highest section of cliff (**site 4**). On a clear day, the views are stunning – a 360-degree panorama starting north at Stac a' Mheadais, then Rum, Canna, South Uist, the coast of Duirinish from the Maidens to Ramasaig, Waternish, Trotternish, bits of the Cuillin – everything you could possibly want to see.

After reaching a freshwater **pool**, the path descends gently and then makes its way around a deep geo guarded by an old fence. From here we crossed a section of **marsh** towards the castle-like buttress – the ancient fortress of Masada set on an impregnable hill – a desert scene with the Roman army holding siege, unable to break through.

As we approached we began to make out the columns. This is what Pennant had come to see. Hardly anyone apart from Nicholas Crane has followed in his footsteps, but here we were, amongst the scree and debris of tumbled rock below the fortress. Some battle had raged here. Geology versus the Elements. Nature versus Nurture. Instinct versus Learning. Calm down. Too excited. Time to read what Pennant actually had to say: "...the ruins of the creation: those of *Rome*, the work of human art, seem to them but as the ruins of yesterday." This is no time to be calm. This is a place to get excited!

When you think of the effort we have to make to reach the Devil's Causeway in County Antrim, or the logistics and uncertainty of making it across to Iona and then by small boat to Staffa; this is as good and as dramatic, and as geologically rare, and yet you have it all to yourself.

We walked up to the base and then followed a narrow sheep track underneath the giant columns. The further south we moved, the more weathered the columns became. The prevailing winds are from the south-east.

We reached the east end of Preshal Beg and followed a short climb up the grass slope separating Preshal Beg and a secondary knoll. At the top of the slope a grassy corridor leads up to the left to become a faint stony path to the top (**site 5**). This is a curious plateau with small rocky pools and a crazed surface, with patches of woolly-hair moss and the occasional fir clubmoss.

Why is there a jumbled layer on top of crisp columns? Geologists call the top layer **'entablature'** whilst the more regular lower zone is referred to as **'colonnade'**. You can see the same zones in Fingal's Cave and the Giant's Causeway. The simplest explanation is that the molten magma was in a thick enough layer to cool slowly into hexagonal prisms whilst the top was suddenly quenched by contact with water, perhaps from a displaced river caused by the moving lava.

We retreated to the grassy corridor and followed its line dropping down to the east side of Preshel Beg. We aimed north over tussocky bilberries and heather followed by an expanse of drainage ditches, deer sedge and bog asphodel. We steered to the right of the right-hand Macleod's Table to reach an isolated **broch** (**site 6**). The outer walls are not as high as the duns at Hallin or Fiadhairt, but the entrance on the east side is impressive with a stone lintel leading to a collapsed gallery. The top is marked by a central cell hidden amongst a jumble of rocks crowned by two elder trees.

The next section requires care in navigation. We aimed off east in the direction of Preshal More and dropped down to follow a line above and parallel with the **Sleadale Burn**, passing two **waterfalls** and crossing a section of **runrig**. There are no clear footpaths here, only the faint suggestion of ancient tracks used by cattle and sheep. The way leads past **gorse** bushes at which point we dropped down to the corner of a fence, which we followed to join the Talisker Bay track.

Notes:

Reference to the after dinner walk to Prieshwell can be found in James Boswell's *The Journal of a Tour to the Hebrides with Samuel Johnson LLD* , Everyman's Library, Dent 1909, p.242

The quotes from Thomas Pennant can be found in *A Tour in Scotland and Voyage to the Hebrides*, 1772. Chester 1774, pp.291-292

Leaning prismatic column on the south-west side of Preshal Beg (Photograph:© Andrew Sharp)

13. Coir a' Mhadaidh

Checklist

Distance	6.2 miles/10km
Approximate time	6 hours
Maps	1:25 000 OS Explorer 411
Terrain	Newly-constructed footpath to the Fairy Pools. River and tributary crossings along the initial section may be difficult after heavy rain. Path to Waterpipe Gully and Coir a' Mhadaidh is less-distinct with sections of loose scree and deeply eroded gullies
Footwear	Boots
Parking	Take the Glenbrittle road and after descending a steep hill through enclosing forestry, look for a car park on the right (NG423258) where the river and the Cuillin ridge come into view

For the occasional hillwalker wishing to visit a Cuillin corrie, the most-likely target is Coire Laggan or Coir a' Ghrunnda. But Coir a' Mhadaidh – the Corrie of the Fox? Where exactly is that? Even with a guide book or map, there is no guarantee you will know exactly where it is!

Old maps and guides placed it to the north of Waterpipe Gully, below Bruach na Frithe. The same maps show Coir a' Tairneilear south of Waterpipe Gully. And then, in one decisive cartographic act, in 1965, the Ordnance Survey switched the names around, and Coir a' Mhadaidh came to lie in the shadow of its namesake – Sgurr a' Mhadaidh.

Climbers and Munro baggers intent on reaching the main ridge are unlikely to include it in their plans, even with the new map. It has no

Water and ice falls above the Fairy Pools

loch and no obvious paths. This is the perfect place to experience the grandness and solitude of the Cuillin, particularly recommended in winter if the tops are out-of-bounds or if you are suffering from a New Year's Day hangover and don't want to meet anybody ever again.

On a frosty January morning, we took the road from Loch Harport to Glenbrittle. The spruce trees along the roadside were covered in hoar frost where the sun had failed to penetrate, but as we approached the edge of the plantation, the branches turned to green. We managed an icy downhill bend before reaching the car park on the right.

Boots on, eat a banana, check gloves, scarf, and away. We were an informal group of four. I was severely handicapped by having to wear my work boots having lent John my only pair of climbing boots for the day.

There was some difficulty crossing two of the stream tributaries but then it was easy walking on a well-made path. The first noticeable feature was a large boulder standing on its own about 20 metres to the right of the path (**site 1**). There is faintly-worn track leading straight to it, indicating a certain level of attention it receives in summer.

Look closely at the vertical east-facing side. It is covered in rock tripe – a lichen found on isolated rocks that have been used as a bird perch. It is often found where there are localised concentrations of nitrogen, such as a flat top or extending down the sides in rain channels. But there was hardly any growing on this top. And why wasn't it growing in the rain channels, apart from on the east-facing side? Could this indicate human behaviour – a favourite rock for scrambling over, perhaps?

We moved on, passed the **Fairy Pools**. I remember swimming here many summers ago. Now, on this perfect winter's day there was nobody about. No, sorry, not tempted. I was too busy taking photos. The path was frozen solid. Some of the foundation stones looked as though they had sunk below the surface when in fact they had remained firm. The illusion was caused by the rest of the path being heaved upwards by the expanding ice.

Water is at its densest at 4° Celsius. As it approaches its freezing point, it expands and eventually forms ice. In the surface layers of soil, water freezes as it pushes upwards through capillaries to form

The 'Peak of the Chanter' and Waterpipe Gully from the Allt Coir' a' Mhadaidh

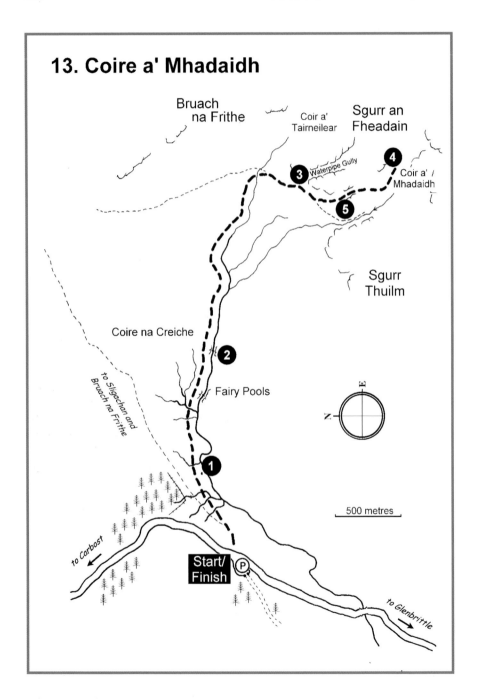

13. Coire a' Mhadaidh

Sites of Interest

1. Large boulder (NG427257)
Distribution of rock tripe influenced by human activity

2. Fairy Pools (NG437255)
Iron oxide flush seeping from peat moorland

3. Waterpipe Gully (NG449248)
One of the three longest gullies in Britain

4. Corrie wall (NG449242)
Waterfalls freeze in winter forming 'ice claws', suggesting diurnal changes in local air flow

5. Lip of corrie (NG446246)
Stone polygons formed in loose scree in winter due to expanding ice crystals

what is called 'needle ice'. Here, we could see it in the path, each needle pushing-up soil and small stones immediately above it.

We arrived at the main pool where a rock bar crosses from side to side. The water draining from the peat moor had run over the edge of the river bank and had frozen into an ice curtain. It had developed a spectacular pattern of coloured stripes caused by localised concentrations of iron oxide in the water (**site 2**).

Iron often seeps out of a peat moor and can be seen on surface water in summer after a dry spell, forming a rainbow of colours like an oil film. The physics is the same. It is caused by diffraction of light through a thin surface film of insoluble ferric hydroxide floating on the surface.

Time for a break. We sat on the side of the path. Not a swimmer in sight. Then on, following the stream with its spectacular part-frozen waterfalls and pools, past the smooth, rounded boulders in the stream bed covered in hoar frost. We follow the stream as it changed its name from Allt Coir' a' Mhadaidh to Allt Coir' a' Tairnealear and crossed over to the right to contour below **Waterpipe Gully (site 3)**.

This gully is special. Ashley Abraham in his book *Rock Climbing in Skye* devotes a whole chapter to it – one of the three longest gullies in Britain, the others being the Chasm on Buchaille Etive Mòr and the Clachaig Gully in Glencoe. The rock climb is 1300ft long with 20 pitches and classed by the SMC guide as Very Severe. It was first climbed in 1895 by Messrs. Kelsall and Hallitt who described it in the Sligachan Climbers' Book as affording "constant interesting, and sometimes difficult climbing." Abraham in his book adds the comment: "it has probably no equal in the British Isles."

The gully runs up the west face of **Sgurr an Fheadain** which is Gaelic for the 'Peak of the Chanters'. Abraham speculates that the name 'Waterpipe' was a mistake, linking it with a pipe through which water is channelled downwards, rather than with 'bagpipes' through which the wind wails as it funnels upwards.

We passed below the base of the gully traversing a section of rough scree. After crossing a stream bed we finally reached the lip of the corrie and entered the fastness of **Coir a' Mhadaidh**.

On that January day we sat and had our lunch near the stream, the focal point of a parabola of crags. The large stones surrounding us had different patterns of hoar frost. Could this depend on the different types of rock, each with different textures and colours affecting the pattern of ice formation?

Higher up the corrie there were a number of rock walls that were covered in ice (**site 4**). Where waterfalls had poured in summer, there hung masses of contorted icicles, some extending horizontally away from the rock in the shape of 'claws'.

On retracing our route out of the corrie we found an area of scree with patterns developing amongst the stones (**site 5**). Repeated freezing and thawing of the ground can produce some strange effects. Geologists refer to 'patterned ground' in which loose surface stones are sorted according to size. On horizontal ground, this can result in the formation of 'stone polygons' where matchbox-size stones are grouped together in lines with finer material accumulating in between.

As we descended the valley, the sun broke through onto the summit of **Bruach na Frithe**. It was the first sun we had seen all day. And with evening drawing in, we passed the Fairy Pools, with still no soul in sight.

Ice claws in Coire a' Mhadaidh

Notes

There has been some recent mathematical work on how icicles tend to grow into a standard shape, like the shape of a stalactite. The idea is that as water runs down the frozen stem to form more ice, a small amount of heat is generated warming the surrounding air which then rises and so keeps the top of the icicle narrower than it would be – hence the long, thin rod shape instead of a stubby knob. But conditions in a Skye corrie are not like those in a laboratory and the wind has its part to play. Here, in Coir' a' Mhadaidh we found all shapes and sizes including 'ice claws', where the updraft had deflected the freezing drops outwards. Some had developed a step-like growth. This could indicate the diurnal wind patterns often generated in a north-facing corrie.

The formation of stone polygons has attracted several explanations. In one theory, the freeze-thaw cycle sets up stresses at the surface similar to what happens when mud cracks into a pattern of hexagons. Ice wedges expand downwards around the margins and force material into the centre of each hexagon to form a shallow mound. The stones brought to the top of these mounds then roll outwards and accumulate at the edges. The smaller stones do not roll as far and so remain near the centre.

Another theory involves the formation of 'needle ice' which was forming typically amongst the loose scree. Ice needles expand and lift or 'heave' the ground surface, pushing stones upwards like a car jack. A thaw will cause the needles to bend and melt and so cast their load of heaved stones down the slope. The larger stones roll further, the smaller stones stay put.

Research experiments have shown that stone patterns can appear after just eight freeze-thaw cycles. Temperatures need only drop to minus five degrees with frost penetrating to a depth of no more than 16-17cm. Such conditions are not unusual in the Scottish hills.

14. Blaven

Checklist

Distance	5 miles/8km
Approximate time	5 to 6 hours
Maps	1:25 000 OS Explorer 411. 1:50 000 British Geological Survey, Sheet 71(W)
Terrain	Steep rough tracks, getting steeper as you get higher with some exposed rock scrambling
Special considerations	Climbing beyond the corrie and onto the ridge is only recommended for the experienced hillwalker
Footwear	Boots
Parking	Large car park at the foot of the Allt na Dunaiche (NG561216)

When you think of the Cuillin, you think of mountains, scrambling, bare rock and scree. Some imagine ropes, abseils and vertigo. You don't think of trees, lush alpines, and carpets of herbs. Where do you walk if you want to sample the natural history without the adrenaline?

Guide books talk of Blaven as being 'a favourite'. Some of the old books say you should only do it with a guide. Others describe a summit that '...may be ascended from Broadford without touching rock'. ('Handbook and Guide to the Misty Isle of Skye' by Kenneth MacRae, published by Duncan MacIntyre, Stationer, Portree, 1921. Price: one shilling and sixpence)

Paths and attitudes change, but one thing is constant: you have to have an eye on the weather. This walk follows the so-called 'easy route' to the top, with the added advantage of offering a get-out clause for the botanist, should the mist come down.

All these years in Skye and never been up Blaven! It was time to put that right. John was the catalyst. He had done the main Cuillin ridge and seemed to think we should be able to manage this 'easy route'.

The weather was reasonably clear with just patches of cloud on the high tops as we arrived at the car park below **Allt na Dunaiche**. The path follows the north bank of the wooded gorge, with no room for error if you put a foot down too far to the left.

The steep sides of this gorge have been extensively surveyed for plants by the John Muir Trust.

We followed the path with views opening out with every step. Look right (**site 1**) and suddenly the V-shaped gap of Strath Mòr leads the eye like a rifle-sight to Dùn Caan on Raasay.

As we gained height above the 200ft contour, the gorge was cut across by several dolerite dykes, leaving steep sided gullies and

Blaven summit in mist!

waterfalls (**site 2**). The one thing about Blaven that separates it from the rest of the Cuillin is the extent of basalt and Jurassic sedimentary rock that make up its flanks. Here on the approach from the east, you are walking over peat but the underlying rocks are **sandstones, shales and limestones** – Jurassic rocks, marked on the geology map as g^{6-9}. The long scarp slope of **An Stac** on the left side of the gorge is composed of **basalt** with dolerite intrusions.

The path crosses the Allt na Dunaiche and bears left, climbing steadily over loose bouldery scree which originates from a seam of **granite** sandwiched between the basalt. The contrast between the acid granite around the path and the fertile crumbling basalt, extending down into the gorge to the left, is remarkable. Basalt looks so green.

Alpine clubmoss in Coire Uaigneach

The climb is relentless, but there are some interesting features where several narrow dolerite dykes cut across the path from south-east to north-west (**site 3**). They cut through both the basalt and granite and can be traced as they continue up to the right. It is these same dykes that form the deep gullies as they cross the **gabbro** ridge.

Alpine lady's mantle in Coire Uaigneach

The terrain becomes more grassy and less steep as you reach the lip of the **Coire Uaigneach**. The crumbling basalt along the north side of the corrie leads to a sudden increase in alpine plants including **Alpine lady's-mantle** and some spectacular creeping stems of **Alpine**

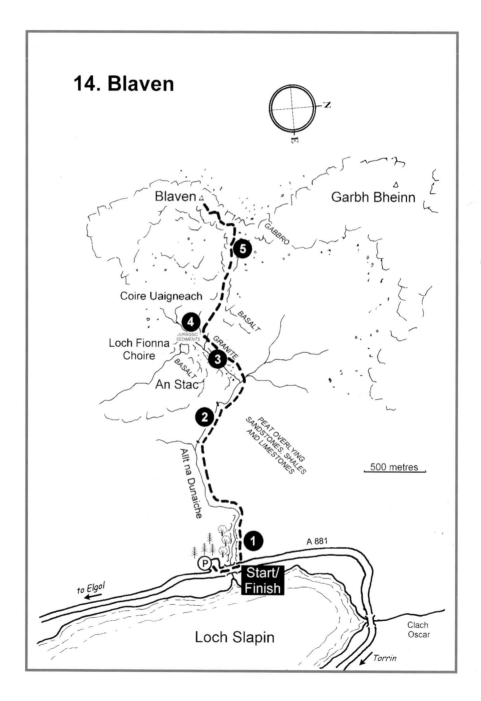

14. Blaven

Sites of Interest

1. **Viewpoint (NG558217)**
   Unusual view of Dùn Caan on Raasay through Strath Mòr

2. **Waterfalls (NG548215)**
   Ravines and waterfalls caused by dolerite dykes crossing
   stream bed

3. **Narrow dykes (NG539214)**
   Swarm of dolerite dykes cutting through basalt, granite and
   gabbro

4. **Alpine flowers (NG536211)**
   Alpine clubmoss and Alpine lady's mantle on crumbling basalt

5. **Rock staircase (NG532215)**
   Path leading to Blaven with rocky sections (and occasional
   banana skins)

clubmoss (site 4). This is where the lichens thrive. This is where the mists come down:

> 'O wondrous mountain of Blaven!
> How oft, since our parting hour,
> You have roared with the wintry torrents,
> You have gloomed through the thunder shower!
> But by this time the lichens are creeping
> Grey-green o'er your rocks and your stones,
> And each afternoon is steeping
> Your bulk in its sultriest bronze.'
> (from Alexander Smith, *A Summer in Skye*)

At this point a decision has to be taken whether to push on to the summit, along a rocky staircase climbing up the east ridge, or to ponder the lichens and alpines in this lush corrie. As John was with us, we packed away the hand-lens in favour of the compass and headed upwards.

Waterfalls on dolerite dykes at site 2

The mist was creeping lower and our senses were spared the views from the shattered vertiginous ridge (**site 5**). But we did notice one thing – a banana skin! This was no metaphor. Someone had just thrown it down on the path. What happened to the maxim 'leave nothing behind but your footprints'?

In a fit of self-satisfied moralizing, we quickly hid the offending litter under a rock to decompose out of sight. Twenty metres further ... yet another. Really, this is just not done. Whoever these people are, they should be taught a lesson and made to clear up after themselves. The second banana skin was gleefully winged off the path to disappear out of sight down a misty ravine. Then a third skin, this one placed on a prominent rock. Who are these people? ... a fourth at the bend in the path ... a fifth where the east ridge joined the summit ridge – each one in turn we ceremoniously dispatched to banana heaven ... and then the sudden realization, in the thickening mist, that this was 'Ariadne's thread' – the line of markers that some astute group had carefully left behind to ensure their safe retreat!

Now we had our own route to negotiate, eventually reaching the summit at the round triangulation column surrounded by a wall of mist. We effected our retreat the same way we had made our ascent, only this time, not quite so smugly.

On the descent, looking across to Loch Fionna Choire

15. Clach Oscar

Checklist

Distance	0.4 miles/0.6km
Approximate time	15 minutes
Maps	1:25 000 OS Explorer 411
Terrain	Level track. Can be muddy after rain
Equipment	Hand-lens
Special considerations	Please do not remove any of the lichens, but leave them for others to enjoy. If you need a record, take a photograph
Footwear	Shoes or sandals, or boots in wet weather
Parking	Off-road section on north-west side of bridge (NG563224) and limited space at start of the route on the east side of the track (NG565224)

Clach Oscar is an important rock. It is even marked on the OS map. It lies alongside what used to be the main road from Broadford to Portree: the route Bonnie Prince Charlie was thought to have taken as he fled from the north to the south of the island.

Park the car near the bridge at the head of Loch Slapin. The path follows the old road and after 200 metres you will have reached Clach Oscar. This is it: the destination; the highlight. No struggle or mountaineering experience required. You could do it in sandals.

What's it all about you ask? It's just a rock in the middle of an empty space, and why are we wasting time down here when we could be enjoying the views on Blaven? Well, if you can do this, you can do it all – but with added spice. After Clach Oscar, walking becomes more than just a physical exercise.

There is something special about approaching a large boulder in the hills for the first time. What you find depends on where you are in the country. If you are near the sea, expect different things than inland. East coast is different from west coast. Is it limestone or granite? More importantly – is it a prominent landmark or one of many rocks close together?

Look closely at this rock. If you were a bird, you would perch here. If you were a sheep you would rub yourself here. As a fellow traveller, you would probably stop and take lunch here. A geologist might even take a rock sample. All this is recorded on this rock.

It used to be bigger but frost and time has split off smaller daughters. It carries the obligatory legend of it being thrown here in anger by a giant. But there is much more ...

One hundred and fifty years ago, the main road from Broadford to Portree ran through Strath Mór. Clach Oscar can be seen to the right of the track

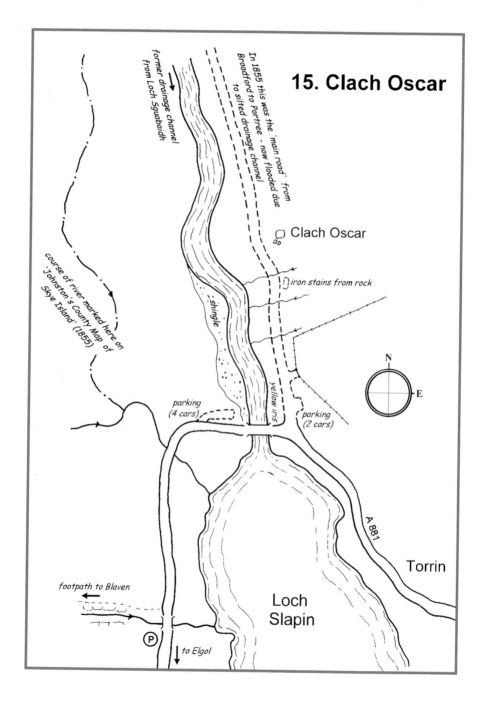

15. Clach Oscar

In 1855 this was the 'main road' from Broadford to Portree - now flooded due to silted drainage channel

former drainage channel from Loch Sguabaidh

course of river marked here on 'Johnston's County Map of Skye Island' (1855)

Clach Oscar

iron stains from rock

shingle

yellow iris

parking (4 cars)

parking (2 cars)

N

E

A 881

Torrin

footpath to Blaven

Loch Slapin

P

to Elgol

Clach Oscar and its split companions

Imagine David Attenborough in that low hushed voice, head half-turned to camera and no sudden movements so as not to disturb his subject. He is sitting here alongside his quarry, accepted as a friend. We watch in awe, realising this is natural history and television history in the making.

We hold on to his every word: "Here in this remote glen ... undisturbed and unknown ... we come across a rare colony ... their silver-grey backs ... often much sought-after in the past as a source of food ... but now protected."

And then he would whisper those magical words: *"Lasallia pustulata!"*

Look closely at the top and sides of this rock. It is covered in lichen, but not your ordinary common-or-garden lichen. This is 'rock tripe' formerly known by the magnificent tongue-twisting scientific name, *Umbilicaria pustulata*, but now answering only to *Lasallia*.

Rock tripe: so lush it seems the rock is giving birth – each offspring attached by an umbilical cord. Rock tripe: silver grey pustules on top with a network of black holes and dimples below, looking for all the world like tripe.

A close encounter with rock tripe

Rock tripe: once used to dye wool a startling mauve but only after adding urine if you really feel you have to; rock tripe that you can eat when you are caught-out in the tundra with no packed lunch and are desperate; rock tripe that turns a livid green and swells in size when wet; rock tripe that follows rain channels running down the rock sides. But most of all – rock tripe *on top*.

Why does it like to be on top? Well, it doesn't take kindly to sheep or people rubbing up against it. It likes sunlight. It's happier on mildly acidic rock. It likes nitrogen, and phosphates. It thrives on bird droppings. That's why it's here. This is a favourite bird perch – the most prominent lookout-site for miles.

Look closely at the top, amongst the lush foliage. See the pellets? The line of guano left by a raven? The jawbone of a vole? The vertebrae of a rabbit? Forget Blaven. Forget the views. For a brief moment of magic, Clach Oscar weaves its spell.

16. Camas Malag

Checklist

Distance	0.6 miles/1km
Approximate time	Could be completed in 1 hour but best take a picnic and make half a day of it
Maps	1:25 000 OS Explorer 411. 1:50 000 British Geological Survey, Sheet 71(W)
Terrain	There are no paths once you have left the main track to Suisnish. Walking over limestone clints and grykes requires concentration
Equipment and books	Hand-lens, torch, sea shore, wildflower and fern guides
Footwear	Boots
Parking	On the A881 Broadford to Elgol road, one mile past Loch Cill Chriosd take the left fork past the marble quarry and continue to the shore where there is parking above the beach (NG582193)

The key to interpreting a landscape often depends on its geology. Here the great rock formations of Skye come together and in a matter of paces, you cross from granite to limestones and then to sandstones and shales. This isn't a gentle mixing. The arrival of molten magma transformed the existing limestones into marble. The forces involved pushed and pulled at the once-horizontal strata leaving vertical faces. Dykes that are normally bounded by parallel walls have been stretched to look like strings of sausages.

On this stage the plants and animals play out their roles. Here, you can observe how geology affects the distribution of plants and animals, as well as influencing animal behaviour. If you thought a limpet was always a limpet, come to Camas Malag.

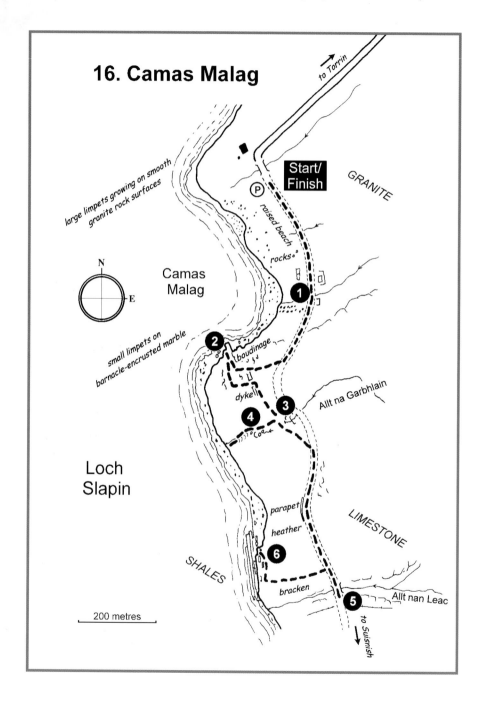

16. Camas Malag

to Torrin

Start/Finish

GRANITE

large limpets growing on smooth
granite rock surfaces

raised beach

rocks

Camas
Malag

N

E

1

small limpets on
barnacle-encrusted marble

2

boudinage

dyke

3

Allt na Garbhlain

4

Coral

Loch
Slapin

parapet

heather

LIMESTONE

6

SHALES

bracken

5

Allt nan Leac

to Suisnish

200 metres

Sites of Interest

1. Ruined buildings (NG583190)
Evidence of former boat shed with boat landing and tie-up posts

2. Marble rock pools (NG583188)
Small limpets suggesting influence of rough rock texture.
Example of dolerite dyke pulled and deformed into sausage-shapes

3. Cave entrance (NG584187)
Disappearing stream in limestone with liverworts and variety of ferns and flowers

4. Stream re-entrant and waterfalls (NG584186)
Two cave openings with green spleenwort and hart's tongue fern

5. Allt na Leac (NG585184)
Patch of mountain everlasting on south side of bridge

6. Jurassic outcrop (NG584184)
Detached rocks with thin wavy strata

We parked the car on granite covered by a 25-foot **raised beach**. It was early morning in May and several groups of visitors had already started out to the deserted village of Suisnish. After a cup of coffee and a sandwich we set off slowly noticing the lush green grass on the tops to several **rocks**.

The ruined buildings at the top of the beach (**site 1**) were made using stones from the shore. You could see the drill holes of various lamellibranches. The ruin without a front wall we surmised was once a boat house. The excitement was in putting together the evidence: the grassy runway leading down to the shore; the rocks that had been arranged as a boat landing; the two wooden posts at the top of the shore that would be just right for tying up – all circumstantial evidence but when taken together the case was overwhelming.

I wanted to check out some rock pools I had seen a few years earlier. They were on a band of limestone next to the granite and so

had been changed to marble (**site 2**). Marble rock pools! That has to be worth checking! What was amazing was the sheer number of barnacles, so tightly packed they were being drawn upwards like skyscrapers. The background rock was a landscape of sharp, crystalline, spiky ridges. Not a flat surface anywhere to lay down a sixpence. On this corrugated razor-edged switch-back lived the limpets. What do you do if you are a limpet and you want to clamp down tight on such a surface? You can do two things: keep moving and don't clamp down or don't grow too large. The larger you are the more difficult it is to find a base.

All the limpets on this marble were small, mostly no more than an inch in diameter. This contrasts with limpets found 400 metres away on the granite shore, many of which were up to two inches across. Limpets start life as males and as they get older and larger they change into females. Does this mean there are more male limpets on marble than on granite?

To the east of the marble rock, a grey cliff supports a brown intrusion of dolerite that has been stretched so that it has narrowed in parts. This type of feature is known to geologists as '**boudinage**' which is derived from the French for a type of sausage.

We scrambled over the dissolving limestone, its clints and grykes with secret caches of wild garlic and hart's tongue fern. Some geologists think the nodules that are weathering out from the rock surface are worm casts but that's debateable.

What do you think, John? No? Unlikely ... depends on whether you lean towards chemistry or biology. At least it's science and not certainty. This was a good time to stop and have another cup of coffee – for some friendly badinage amongst the boudinage.

A grassy corridor led us through a gap in a **dyke** to reach the high point on the track. At the **Alt na Garbhlain** we dropped down to where it poured over a rock edge with a rowan backed by ivy. The stream disappeared under the ground and alongside was the opening of a low cave (**site 3**). Just inside the entrance we found *Conocephalum*, herb robert, wood sorrel, maidenhair spleenwort and celandine. John says it goes in a good distance but I'm not going in there.

The stream flowed underground until it reappeared 50 metres further down in a wonderful fairy dell with an arch over an underground waterfall, and two more cave entrances (**site 4**), the right-

Crossing the eroded limestone towards site 2 with Blaven in the distance

hand one containing hart's tongue fern and green spleenwort. We followed the track of the hidden stream, for curiosity, to see its emergence at the shore at another waterfall.

We retraced our steps and rejoined the main track at its highest point and followed the gentle decent to a concrete **parapet**. Fifty metres past the parapet, looking straight down to the shore, a section of horizontal strata reared up towards us and would have covered us but for it being long-since eroded away. This was the first signs of the Jurassic sandstone and shale. You can see where it lies hidden – where the ground is covered in **heather** and bracken. In contrast, the limestone that we were leaving behind is bare and grey, like wrinkled elephant skin.

above: The view across Camas Malag to Sgurr nan Each and Belig
left: 'Boudinage' (above site 2) takes its name from the French word
for sausage

We reached the **Alt na Leac** at a concrete bridge (**site 5**) where we found a patch of mountain everlasting. And that's as far as we went. Everyone else was rushing full speed ahead to complete the circuit to Suisnish and back, with no time to stand and stare, no time for looking down.

We turned back and after 60 metres from the bridge dropped down left along a faint path through **bracken**. This took us to the Jurassic outcrop (**site 6**). This is part of the Upper Broadford Beds. Bright green grass on top is always worth checking for spraints or bird pellets. The detached sections of rock further above the shore had horizontal wavy strata in which grew a few sprigs of wall rue. The nettles below indicated this was a favourite shelter for sheep. And on top sat a hawthorn showing the prevailing wind direction. Perfect!

17. Elgol

Checklist

Distance	2 miles/3.2km
Approximate time	This is not a walk to be rushed. Allow 2 to 3 hours
Maps	1:25 000 OS Explorer 411. 1:50 000 British Geological Survey, Sheet 71(W)
Terrain	Easy gradients on faint paths over heather moor. Rough boulders and pebbles on shore
Equipment and books	Hand-lens, torch, wildflower and sea shore guides
Special considerations	Care required on coastal path to avoid hidden gullies and sink holes. Check with tide tables the best times to explore the shore
Footwear	Boots
Parking	Various parking places before reaching the jetty (NG515135) and up the hill above the shore (NG518135)

Elgol draws the eye to the Cuillin. You arrive at the jetty and you think of the boat trip to Coruisk or you gaze up to the ridiculously-sharp peak of Garsbeinn knowing that it's the start of the Cuillin ridge – but not today. Today you arrive at the jetty and turn left.

This is a comparatively quiet section of coast. Hardly anyone comes here just to look at the sea shore. Those that do turn their back on the Cuillin have their mind set on reaching Prince Charles's Cave. This walk defies such thoughts. Turn left at Elgol and the whole shore is yours.

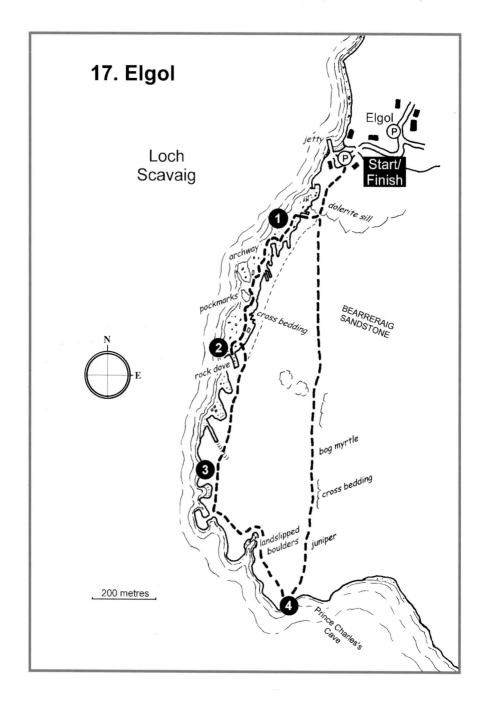

17. Elgol

Loch Scavaig

Elgol

jetty

Start/Finish

dolerite sill

archway

pockmarks

cross bedding

BEARRERAIG SANDSTONE

rock dove

bog myrtle

cross bedding

landslipped boulders

juniper

N

E

200 metres

Prince Charles's Cave

Sites of Interest

1. **Rocky shore (NG513132)**
   Sandstone cliffs, gullies and platforms with wild garlic, sea spleenwort and otter sprainting sites.

2. **Rock cleft (NG5141332)**
   Narrow cave and water curtain with nesting rock doves

3. **Cliff-top gullies (NG513126)**
   Series of narrow gullies with detached stack and nesting fulmar

4. **Headland (NG515124)**
   View of shore and Prince Charles's Cave

"A bit further, Mike... Perfect! Could be the cover photo!"

We set off south from the **jetty** after taking the obligatory photo of the Cuillin skyline looking north over Loch Scavaig. A narrow path left the road and climbed onto the boggy moor. Nothing exciting yet until we reached the edge of the **dolerite sill**. Now the path dropped down onto what is known as **Bearreraig Sandstone**. The path to Prince Charles's Cave faithfully follows the low cliff edge. We ignored it and picked our way down to the shore at the first line of weakness, passing the first sunken cleft. If this was limestone I would be saying clints and dykes. But the geology map insists this is sandstone (**site 1**).

It's difficult to know where to turn. This shore is just brimming with wonderful things: a rowan by a waterfall; a gully with wild garlic, primroses, wood sage, wood rush and bilberries; round a corner to a fairy grotto with sea spleenwort and crowberry. Are you sure this isn't Durness Limestone? And look – you're missing all this – otter – look it's otter. You've missed an otter-dropping, Mike. Look – green grass, a bit darker; and then another gully with English stonecrop. Astonishing!

We must have been an hour poking around corners, gully after gully, one with an **archway**. Amazing! Shaded rock faces with ivy and wood sage and bluebells, violets, and oystercatchers calling close by. Fantastic lichens and rocks glistening like crystalline sugar. Liverworts and mosses. A chaotic jumble of blocks and slabs with intrusions of dolerite through the sandstone. And the sudden realisation that this is what was causing the gullies, all trending in the same direction – south-east to north-west. And we hadn't even begun to look at the rock pools full of sea anemones.

The slabs on the shore had **pock marks** and basin-shaped hollows, similar to what you find on the millstone grit of the Pennines. The vertical faces of the cliffs at the top of the shore had what geologists describe as **'trough cross bedding'**. Here were ripple marks half-a-metre-high left by sea currents moving in a north-westerly direction in shallow water, 160 million years ago.

We had barely gone a mile and yet two hours had flown by. Time for lunch and to photograph an amazing volcanic intrusion that tapered to a point. Then it was round the next corner into a narrow-walled rock cleft (**site 2**), through a curtain of water, over a thick matt of rotting seaweed and slippery rounded pebbles, and into darkness. A **rock dove** flew out. John had a head torch and was able to make-

Cross bedding in the Bearreraig Sandstone on the return path across the moor

The start of the walk at the Elgol jetty

out two nests high above. The floor below had two heaped piles of guano indicating these were established nests that were used year after year.

From here we retraced our steps to a gap in the cliff to regain the path through the heather to Prince Charles's Cave. Gully after gully followed, with deeper and deeper chasms and clefts with views down to the shore (**site 3**). The scenery was getting more dramatic: one, two, three, four gullies. Number four was just a metre wide. We passed another narrow inlet – call it number five. Can this get more dramatic? Yes, because number six leads to a narrow neck leading to what is about to become a detached stack, and number seven has already become detached. This is not the place to be in a strong offshore wind or in mist or twilight. But at any other time this is the place to be!

After the headland with its wheeling fulmar the rest could only be anticlimax, but we still continued following the path as it traced its way around the edge of a large indent with **landslipped boulders** at its head, on to a headland where we caught our first glimpse of the Prince's Cave (**site 4**). "Too far!" we all agreed, and the tide was wrong anyway. And so we followed the faint track back across the heather, back to Elgol and the car park.

18. Tokavaig

Checklist

Distance	1.1 miles/1.8km
Approximate time	30 minutes to 1 hour
Maps	1:25 000 OS Explorer 412
Terrain	Level road and grassy foreshore
Equipment and books	Hand-lens. Lichen identification guide
Special considerations	Please avoid removing or damaging any of the *Lobarion* lichens or hazelgloves fungus. Leave only footprints: take only photos
Footwear	Boots or walking shoes
Parking	Roadside verge (NG597117)

You somehow fall upon Tokavaig. It's suddenly there in the mid-section of the Ord Tarskavaig loop road. Most visitors will stop here for a quick photo of Dunscaith Castle and the view across to Rum and Blaven. But they miss the hazelwoods.

This is one of those rare sites that has had a continuous covering of woodland for over 10,000 years, since the land became colonized after the last Ice Age. This is not scrub woodland. This is the remains of the wild wood that once covered most of north-west Scotland. Its branches are covered in rare lichens and fungi. Almost everyone passes it by without a second glance, but today is different.

We parked on the close-cropped grass verge in front Òb Gauscavaig. It's hard to resist doing what everyone does when you have a view like that. Window down, camera out, wait for the sun to be just right and – Snap! – Dunscaith Castle, with its round portal underneath that gateway.

This is a place that is at its most atmospheric early evening, early summer. The low sun strikes the branches of the hazel which now

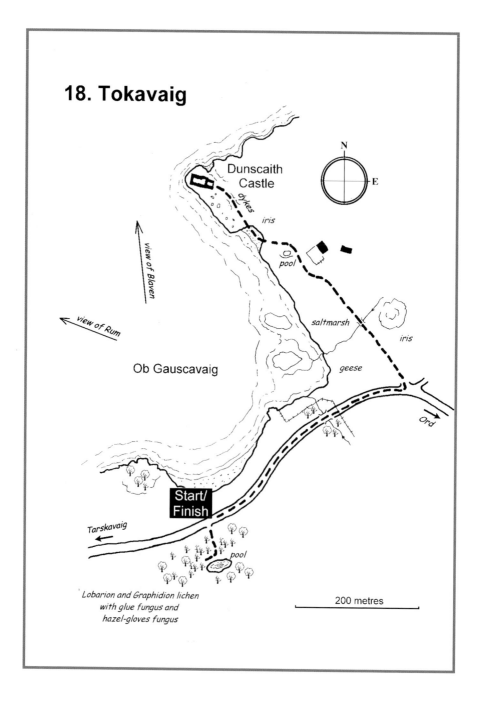

18. Tokavaig

Dunscaith Castle

N
E

dykes

iris

pool

view of Blaven

view of Rum

saltmarsh

iris

Ob Gauscavaig

geese

Ord

Start/ Finish

Tarskavaig

pool

Lobarion and Graphidion lichen
with glue fungus and
hazel-gloves fungus

200 metres

stand out against the dark interior like bleached bones. It's odd to think that this is hazel, the tree that gave its name to the colour brown. After all, hazel bark is usually brown.

But this is not the usual hazel. Old age and Atlantic winds have taken their toll. You are not seeing the bark, for it is hidden under a patina of ancient script lichen; lichens that are called 'smoothies' or the *Graphidion* by those in the know; lichens that look like hieroglyphics written on parchment; lichens with Latin names like *Graphis scripta*; lichens to be found only in north-west Scotland, and lichens that are predominantly white.

We ventured a little deeper into the wood coming face to face with the *Lobarion* group with all its fearful Latin names. Then a twig appeared as if glued to a stem, held by a fungus in its black putty-like grip. *Hymenochaete corrugate*. Once you see that, there is always a chance of finding the hazel-gloves fungus, or 'troll hand' as it's called

Dunscaith Castle

'white bones' of the ancient hazelwood at Tokavaig

in Sweden, like a bright orange rubber glove grabbing hold of the branch.

The light was fading and so we quickly paid our respects to Dunscaith Castle. Greylag geese took flight from grazing the salmarsh, and sandpipers were calling continuously as we followed the faint track towards the castle entrance. A series of volcanic dykes led us in a south-east to north-west direction, making a natural line of approach. A few more photos in twilight and then it was back to the car and the deserted road.

'Trollhand' or hazelgloves fungus

19. Leitir Fura

Checklist

Distance	4.9 miles/7.9km
Approximate time	3 hours
Maps	1:25 000 OS Explorer 413
Terrain	Un-surfaced forest roads and well-maintained drovers' path
Footwear	Boots
Parking	When travelling on A851 from Broadford to Armadale, take the narrow forestry track left (just after the Drumfearn turn-off). Sign: Leitir Fura. The large car park (NG704162) is approximately 1 mile down the un-metalled track

The choice of where to walk in Skye is often governed by the season and the weather. The walk through the woods to Leitir Fura is one that can be done anytime: in mid-winter when the lack of daylight and icy conditions make the Cuillin difficult; in high summer when you seek the cool shade; in driving rain because it is sheltered, or like I remember, in early November to celebrate Janet's birthday at Kinloch Lodge – hopping about on one leg after the walk in near-dark conditions, changing out of mud-spattered overtrousers into a suit and tie in a thankfully-deserted car park before the meal.

Early May: cumulonimbus clouds and we had forgotten the umbrella. Many years had passed since our last visit here. We turned off the Broadford-Armadale road at the sign to Leitir Fura and followed a rough track for a mile before reaching the car park. After yet another heavy shower, we set off along the forest road that leads to the deserted village of Leitir Fura.

A gentle climb bordered by an interminable line of young birch and willow led us past a few fence posts on the left, past a small lay-by with a brief view across Loch na Dal. Sixty more metres and we reached a gate, a kissing gate which I managed to squeeze through and bang my camera. Path levels off, with a big **sessile oak** tree on the left. Path drops down, with some interesting roles of rylock in a lay-by on the left and Janet has just told me to cheer up and not to be so cynical.

What you see depends on your attitude. You can tear off at 3mph and have a good workout and see nothing. Or you can slow down and take-in the detail ... bog myrtle and woodrush on the right; over a stream, hard fern and heather and bluebells; a stump of birch on the edge of the path with a fan-shaped bracket fungus with beautiful blue and mauve parallel bands (***Trametes versicolor***); forty metres further – a quarry on left; over a culvert and then the first hazel on right. Slow down. This isn't a race ... another quarry, then over a stream with a waterfall hidden with **rowans**; and then, after another 80 metres you reach the start of the narrow drovers' path (**site 1**).

This is where it starts to get interesting.

Old hazel stools are always interesting. Here they border the path and are covered in old forest lichens, collectively known as 'the Lobarion'. Four species are quite rare: 'tree lungwort', (*Lobaria pulmonaria*),

Glue fungus at the side of the drovers' path

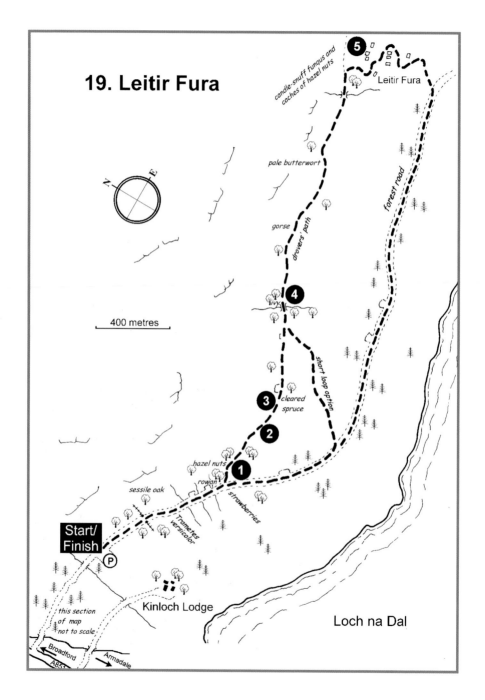

19. Leitir Fura

candle-snuff fungus and
caches of hazel nuts

Leitir Fura

5

forest road

pale butterwort

N · E

drovers' path

gorse

400 metres

4
ivy

short loop option

3
cleared
spruce

2

hazel nuts

1

rowan

sessile oak

strawberries

Trametes
versicolor

Start/
Finish

(P)

Kinloch Lodge

Loch na Dal

this section
of map
not to scale

Broadford

Armadale

A851

Sites of Interest

1. **Drovers' path (NG712154)**
   Old hazel with *Lobarion* lichens

2. **Information post (NG714154)**
   Sprainting site for pine martens and otters in middle of path

3. **Old hazel (NG716154)**
   Glue fungus attaching dead twigs to live stems

4. **Isolated boulder (NG721155)**
   Bilberries, crowberries and reindeer lichens growing on
   sandstone boulder

5. **Ruined walls with holly tree (NG731159)**
   Moss, lichen and candle-snuff fungus. Tracks of woodmice
   with caches of hazel nuts

'green satin lichen' (*Lobaria virens*), 'plum-fruited felt lichen' (*Degelia plumbia*); not forgetting 'blobby jelly-skin lichen' (*Leptogium brebissonii*) – who could forget?

Some of the broken twigs are stuck to others with glue fungus. Some of the better-lit side branches are covered in *Polypody* ferns and almost all the inner shaded stems are colonised by purple liverwort. Fantastic!

Hidden away at the base of these hazel stools, in dry pockets of grass, are the remains of **hazel nuts**, stored here in secret by a wood mouse. They have the tell-tale teeth marks: tiny parallel scratches in groups of two left by the lower incisors.

The sun was now streaking through the undergrowth making the bluebells and the scaly male fern look magnificent. The path climbed and dipped. Every time it dipped there seemed to be a patch of hazel. Where it climbed it was mostly birch. Every hazel had *Lobarion* lichens: every birch had beard-like *Usnea* lichens. Hazel is less acid; birch is more acid. That's what makes the lichens interesting. It's like walking through a wood draped in litmus paper.

When we last came here, about ten years ago, the next section was a tunnel of Sitka spruce with no views and hardly any light. Now, the conifers had been felled and the views across **Loch na Dal** were a complete surprise. Now you can look south to the lighthouse on Isleornsay framed between the occasional birch, and north to the cloud-dappled mountains at the head of Loch Hourn.

We approached one of the first of several information posts with its flip-up sign. In front of this post, in the middle of the path, were two piles of animal faeces, often referred to as 'scats' or 'spraints' (**site 2**). One looked oily black and was studded with beetle carapaces. The other was more like something the cat had sicked-up – pale yellow and studded with what looked like orange lentils – possibly from a

A view of Loch na Dal and the Isleornsay lighthouse through the scattered birch

pine marten or perhaps an otter that had been eating shrimps along the sea shore.

It may seem ridiculous to specify a particular spot on a path to look for droppings but these animals are territorial and they often leave their mark in a conspicuous spot time after time. I remember once seeing some fox droppings where an old stone wall crossed a footpath. On revisiting the site after a gap of eight years, the droppings were still there – different droppings, perhaps a different fox, but exactly the same site!

When it comes to animal behaviour, it is remarkable how regular it can be. A roebuck will fray the bark off the same tree to mark the boundary of its territory. Otters will regularly cut across the same bend in a stream and leave a track. Minke whales will often be seen following the same line of swirling water, the same distance out from the shore, caused by a tidal race. A kestrel will sit on the same plucking post.

It reminds me of when I used to take guests on guided walks at the back of our croft. I'd be looking down intently through a magnifying glass at some sundew or something, and out of the corner of my eye would happen to see a small dark blob in silhouette on the skyline, over a mile away. "Buzzard!" I would say, to gasps of amazement, pointing casually with an outstretched finger over to my left, without even bothering to look. The male buzzard was always sitting there on its favourite perch – but of course I kept that secret!

The path now drops down a little with great views of Loch na Dal, past a rock with folded strata on the left side of the path; two metres further – a hazel with more glue fungus (**site 3**). More views of lighthouse over **cleared spruce**. More gentle drops and rises, past a second quarry on left. (The *Polytrichum* moss on each side of path reminds me of the last time we were here, on that wet November day, when this was completely overshadowed by spruce, and the moss was all that was growing.) The path now climbs gently. More spraints. Oak and mature birch on left. Then at the top, a wooden seat and 60 metres further, the return **short-loop option** turns back to the right.

The long-loop option continues along the drovers' path. After a further 200 metres you cross a wooden footbridge. Notice the ivy growing over a holly tree. The mature leaves are quite different in shape from the young leaves. You pass an area of birch and then cross a small stream. Look for an isolated boulder on the right of the path

Green satin lichen on hazel

(**site 4**). Here you will find bilberries, crowberries and several reindeer lichens.

The route continues across open hillside with patches of **pale butterwort** growing near the drainage ditch to the left of the path. After crossing a footbridge, a path leaves the old drovers' route and drops down to the village of **Leitir Fura**. An information board shows the history of the village and its layout.

One ruin in particular deserves a close inspection. As you descend the path, look ahead and to the left for a large holly tree growing out from one of the walls (**site 5**). Look carefully further along the wall for a sawn-off rowan stump supporting inch-high black filaments of **candle-snuff fungus**. Look also for narrow passages or runs made by woodmice leading to hidden **caches of hazel nuts**.

The path drops through the village to join the **forest road** which takes you back to your starting point at the car park

20. Point of Sleat

Checklist

Distance	5.3 miles/8.5km
Approximate time	5 to 6 hours
Maps	1:25 000 OS Explorer 412
Terrain	Dry land-rover track for the first half and then a narrow path over peat and straggly heather – wet and slippery in places
Equipment	Binoculars
Special considerations	Don't underestimate the distance and allow plenty of time
Footwear	Boots treated with plenty of wax
Parking	Parking area at road end, Aird of Sleat (NG588007)

Point of Sleat is the place for the serious birdwatcher. This is one of those headlands that sea birds just have to fly past as they move back and forth to their feeding grounds. Sit below the lighthouse and scan the sea surface and there they go – Manx shearwaters, still to be found in groups of a hundred or more, skimming the waves, tilting and gliding, their black backs turning to white, circuit after circuit, like a fairground carousel.

This is not a walk to rush. The moment you turn off the main road from the Armadale ferry – along the quiet single-track, past Ardvasar, along winding bends and dips and climbs, past glades of oak and sheltered streams – you have to slow down. For all those frantic executives with deadlines to meet, this is where the rehabilitation begins. This is how life used to be before the motorway, before the world went mad.

The walk starts at the road end. A gate marks the start of a well-made track with superb views along the Sound of Sleat and across to Mallaig.

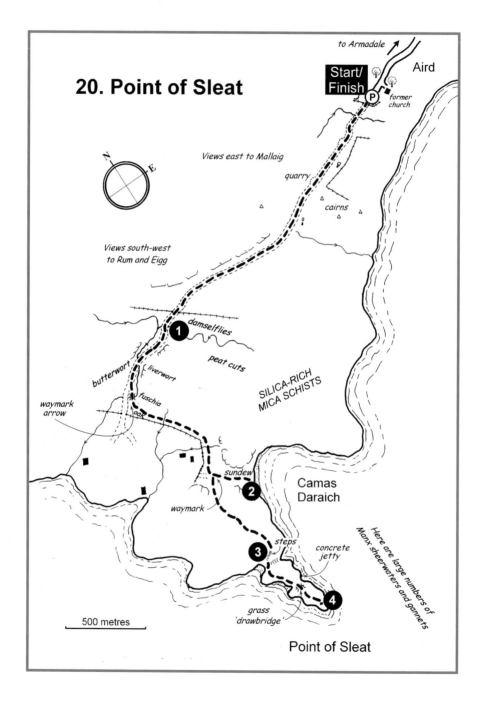

20. Point of Sleat

Sites of Interest

1. Converging streams (NG572004)
Wetland area with dragonflies, bog myrtle and pond weeds

2. Camas Daraich (NG566998)
Sandstone coves, insectivorous plants, white sandy beach

3. Steps (NG562995)
Surface erosion of concrete caused by acids from peat and mica schist

4. Lighthouse (NG562991)
Sea-watching site for gannets and Manx shearwaters

After passing a small **quarry** on the right, the track climbs gently to reach a high point with magnificent views south to Rum and Eigg.

A steady descent leads through a gate into an area of converging streams (**site 1**) with bog myrtle and various pond weeds. Look closely along this section for red **damselflies** and dragonflies.

After passing a waterfall, keep a lookout for a vertical wall of rock on the right of the track covered in **butterwort**. These green starfish-like leaves are flooded in sticky fluid which traps and dissolves any small insect that lands upon it. On the left of the track, the stream

Butterwort growing on vertical rock face alongside the Land-rover track

At the start of the walk looking east along the coast towards Aird

banks are lined with liverwort.

One hundred metres further you cross a footbridge with fuchsias and roses growing alongside. A waymark arrow points the way left, up a narrow stony path which climbs under a **sessile oak** covered in polypody fern. The path now follows a wire fence. This section can be very rutted and slippery after rain, crossing several areas of eroded peat.

The path continues following the fence and then cuts down left to the shore along a grassy hollow. The folded strata of sandstones and mica form an impressive cliff across to your left. **Waymark** arrows point down to the shore and across to the right towards the lighthouse.

The shore is worth exploring. There are many coves and cracks at the back of the low cliffs with liverworts and wood sorrel (**site 2**). In front is an unexpected area of sphagnum with the insect-eating **sundew**, like miniature table tennis bats covered in sticky 'hairs'. But the main attraction is the beach: white sand leading into a turquoise-blue sea.

The track to the lighthouse starts back at the waymark and leads over straggly heather before dropping down to the grassy platforms, canyons and coves that characterize this headland.

After descending a rocky section, you follow a series of concrete **steps** with a guide rope conveniently placed alongside (**site 3**). The acid nature of the mica schist combined with peat produces surface water that is extremely acid. It has dissolved the cement from the concrete, leaving the gravel base behind.

Journey's End: the lighthouse at Point of Sleat

You enter a short grassy valley which leads onto the shore, with shingle and driftwood and oystercatchers calling, past a concrete jetty on the left, over what could be a grass 'drawbridge' to finally arrive at the **lighthouse (site 4)**.

Now it's time to find that flat rock, take out the binoculars, and while-away the afternoon ...

Also from Sigma Leisure:

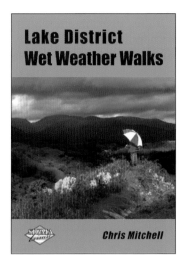

Lake District Wet Weather Walks
Chris Mitchell
There are hundreds of guide books on the Lake District but none of them deals specifically with the problem of where to walk and what to see in wet weather. After some of the wettest summers on record, 20 walks have been chosen to cover all regions of the Lake District so that you will be able to try them out wherever you happen to be when the weather closes in.
£7.99

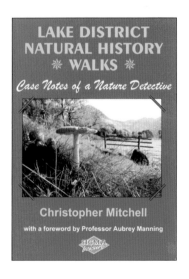

Lake District Natural History Walks
Case Notes of a Nature Detective
Christopher Mitchell
18 walks suitable for all ages and abilities
Fascinating facts help you interpret the country- side by looking at the effects of geology and plant life on the animal population of the area.
£8.95

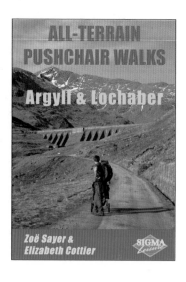